Legacy Prayers

Reflecting His Image

by
Becky Reagan

authorHOUSE

AuthorHouse™
1663 Liberty Drive
Bloomington, IN 47403
www.authorhouse.com
Phone: 833-262-8899

Published by AuthorHouse 03/19/2024

ISBN: 978-1-4259-8421-2 (sc)

Library of Congress Control Number: 2007901504

Print information available on the last page.

TABLE OF CONTENTS

PREFACE

MY HEART LONGS TO leave a meaningful legacy to my children and their heirs. It must be one that will maintain its value through time. It must have the capacity to add quality, meaning and purpose to their lives. It must communicate the huge amount of passion in my heart for those little eyes and ears, hands and feet. And above all, it must honor God.

Legacy Prayers – Reflecting His Image is a collection of my experiences and the truths I've gleaned from the word of God over the years. Hopefully it will become a worn out handbook, read and re-read, underlined and highlighted as God ministers and his image is revealed.

If you're broken or abused or can't find your purpose, this book is for you. If your life is a blessing but you long for a more powerful prayer life, this book is for you. If you've never prayed because you don't know what to say, this book is for you.

God has a legacy for *you*. It is his story. It is his plan for an intimate relationship with you, but how can you have a relationship with God if you don't know him?

Our lives of total chaos are so crammed with busy schedules and agendas we're oblivious to the invisible, spiritual world around us. We have no time to wonder how many gods there are, or if there are any. Prayer isn't taught in schools nor allowed in most public places. Yet when disaster strikes, we're all on our knees begging for protection from the God who has all authority and power to intercede, solve our problems, and change our lives.

There is one true and living God who loves you unconditionally and has laid down his life for you. His name is YHVH in Hebrew. He is the God of Abraham, Isaac, and Jacob. His word is written for our instruction – a light to lead us through a dark world.

And then there is the god of this world, whose name is Lucifer. His days are numbered and he will do whatever it takes to distract you from learning about, and building a powerful relationship with YHVH.

And so the battle begins. It is the battle for your soul – your life. <u>You</u> are the target! Your protection and victory depends totally upon your relationship with YHVH. How do you build that relationship? We call it prayer.

Prepare for the battle or become a casualty!

Listen, my children, to words from above;

Filled with His goodness, filled with His love.

Come to His table prepared to receive

Peace and protection – come, just believe.

When your heart pounds with fear

From abuse and pain

Come to the Healer – Jesus Christ is His name.

Lift up your voice to the Father above

Ask Him into your heart – to fill it with love.

In the darkest of nights and everyday storms

There's only *one* safe house to keep you from harm.

Embrace it; run to it, be restored and refreshed

Abide in His word and your soul will be blessed!

All scripture is given by inspiration of God and is profitable for doctrine, for reproof, for

correction, and for instruction in righteousness, that the man of God may be perfect,

thoroughly furnished unto all good works.

2 Tim 3:16-17 KJV

Prayer Foundations

The most desperate prayer in my life took place the day our 4 month old son was sent home to die. After 14 days in intensive care, the doctors confessed nothing more could be done and with soft, sympathetic voices, asked if we would like to take him home. Today he is the associate pastor at a large church in Louisville, Kentucky, with a heart for God and a passion to teach God's word to people.

Prayer is powerful. Prayer brings renewal. Prayer improves lives. Prayer is conversation and communication with God. Prayer is thanksgiving and praise and worship. Prayer is a search for wisdom and direction. Prayer is pleading for help when we have no answers, or when the answers, *or even the questions,* don't make any sense. Some prayers are answered immediately. Others go unanswered for years. Prayer is an enigma – mysterious, baffling and unexplainable.

Prayer is conversation with God. There are as many prayers as there are conversations and, while some are more effective than others, whether or not you receive an answer may depend upon the condition of your heart and how well you understand your purpose, or your role. And then again sometimes God answers your prayers, *or not,* because of someone else's prayers for you, or just because he simply loves you!

You inherited power from God that not only can improve the quality of your life and the lives of others, but can also draw you into a close personal relationship with God. That power is in God's living word and when used in conversation with him, you will be refreshed, renewed, revived and rescued. We call it prayer. And that's what this book is about.

If one thousand people standing by the Grand Canyon at the same time were asked to *describe the Grand Canyon,* would any two of the descriptions be the same? So it is with prayer.

If the same people were asked to *describe the clouds* in the sky as they looked at the Grand Canyon, again, would any two be alike? In describing the clouds, the sky adds a new *dimension* since, unlike the canyon, it is constantly changing. So it is with prayer.

If the same people were asked to *describe how they felt* as they watched the clouds in the sky as they looked at the Grand Canyon, would any two be alike? So it is with prayer.

Yet at the feet of God prayer sets spiritual actions in motion. Does it really matter who or how one defines it? Does it really matter whether one understands it?

God calls upon his prayer warriors to pray for his people in need. God may awaken a prayer warrior in the middle of the night in the one part of the world to pray for someone in desperate need in a totally different part of the world. That person may be hundreds or thousands of miles away and rarely will the prayer warrior know the importance, or end result, of that prayer. We know there is a great deal of power within these prayers; our challenge is to find and unleash that power.

But how do you put so much faith in something you cannot see? How do you dare to believe someone loves you so much he would give up all he has to buy you back from the slavery of sin and draw you into a close, personal, eternal relationship with him?

Even though it's very difficult to define *or* understand prayer *(let alone understand why God would want to build a relationship with such sinful people)*, there are foundations and effects we can learn about prayer to help us understand how it works and why.

In order to build a more effective, results-oriented conversation with God, several elements must be understood. We'll call these *prayer foundations*. You need a knowledge base to understand God's story; an intimate relationship with God to understand your purpose and your role in his story; an awareness of the ongoing spiritual battle taking place, and an understanding of the power you've been given through the image in which you were created. These powerful foundations will enable you to come to him boldly in prayer with confidence and passion and fill your heart with peace beyond your wildest dreams.

Come to speech class. Learn what God wants to hear. Listen to what he has to say. Train to be his mighty warrior while he develops your spirit to stand, your heart to love, and your words to fight the invisible battle.

God is real, beloved. He is your Father! He longs to hear your voice, to listen to your hopes, your dreams, and your plans. His passion for you will never end. He wants to meet you every morning and walk with you all day, to share the hope he's promised, to fulfill your dreams, and to unfold the awesome plans he has for your life.

A father knows what his kids mean to him. A child knows what his father means to him. *You* are that child. Spend time with your Father! Ask him to become the best part of your life. Let him teach you and train you gently, and lovingly, as only a father can.

<table>
<tr><td>

DIRT

</td><td>

"Then the LORD God formed the man from the dust of the ground. He breathed the breath of life into the man's nostrils, and the man became a living person."

Genesis 2:7 AMPC

</td></tr>
</table>

We all started out as dirt; just a lumpy ball of clay. In order for God to make us into beautiful, useful vessels for his purpose, it is necessary for him to roll us around, thump on us, push and squeeze, pinch and pull, spin us, mold us, and then shove us into hot fires. Then he paints us with a beautiful design and shoves us into the fire again.

Just as he molds and shapes our hearts and minds, so also he longs to mold our mouths around his words, that we would speak powerful, effective, healing prayers to comfort, feed, and shelter the multitudes, leading them from their insecurity into his presence to let him capture their hearts.

How does he do it? Prayer.

Prayer is one of those calming, comfortable, *volatile* words - quite similar to being prepared for battle, and then attacked by surprise. When you're prepared to pray, when you trust your commander explicitly and know your role in his army, when you've been through his "boot camp" and have memorized the strategies, when you grasp what it is you need from God and understand how to attain it, a calming, peaceful presence flows through your entire being, defeating the enemy and ministering to the wounded.

You become the beautiful vessel. But not without disciplined training to work through and overcome the pain and suffering, trials and fires of life; not without constant study and memorization of your commander's precepts and strategies.

It takes months of planning, training and execution to prepare military forces to battle the enemy. Military leaders *must* build a confident, trusting relationship with their warriors and be able to teach their troops comprehensive details of the enemy's capabilities. Strategies and historical data must be studied and reviewed repeatedly.

Military leaders must also thoroughly understand their warriors. They *must* know what's on their minds and in their hearts. They *must* understand what motivates them to be driven to sacrifice and obedience, as well as what problems and limitations need to be met, and resolved, in order to attain solid judgment with clarity and boldness.

To win any battle, it is *critical* to spend huge amounts of time preparing troops not only physically, but also mentally, spiritually and emotionally because the enemy is *determined* to destroy us.

And so it is with prayer.

If you're thinking that's too much work, you must also know the military doesn't send civilians into battle, although civilians are often left wounded and helpless when the battle hits too close to home.

Countries without a military presence are either run over and conquered or left alone because they emit no threat. If you're a prayer civilian, and not a prayer warrior, you also risk being overtaken by the enemy.

Perhaps that's what it comes down to -- deciding to be a civilian, whose future is in someone else's hands, or a warrior of the Almighty God.

Warriors, where do we begin?

We have a comfort zone in asking for prayer, or offering to pray, particularly in devastating conditions with life-threatening circumstances. Even the *word* "prayer" brings a calm assurance we're in God's hands and all will turn out well. But outside of tragedy or catastrophe, we're off our guard. We're so accustomed to God's grace we simply don't train for the battle.

> *"Put on the full armor of God, so that you will be able to stand firm against the schemes of the devil. For our struggle is not against flesh and blood, but against the rulers, against the powers, against the world forces of this darkness, against the spiritual forces of wickedness in the heavenly places. Therefore, take up the full armor of God, so that you will be able to resist in the evil day, and having done everything, to stand firm."*
> *Ephesians 6:11-13 NASB*

PREPARE FOR BATTLE

What we see is not always as it seems. We are spiritual people in a physical world and, without insight into God's word and his vision for our lives, we have a tough time understanding our purpose.

We are at war! God is our general. He has given specific tools and instructions in his manual – his story – to make us strong warriors to protect those we love. We can either train up in the way he knows will prosper us, or we can choose our own rules.

If you're comfortable making up your own rules, great. If you'd like a little more information in a few areas, please check out the power and authority God has given you; the relationship he longs to build with you; and the fire power available to you through prayer.

Within the next few chapters we'll check out God's story – but only a brief overview. You'll find the unabridged version in the Holy Bible. It's a great true story that began thousands of years ago. Interestingly, *you* are one of the main characters – with a special performing role in God's story!

We all love a great story – a bit of chivalry, danger, romance, betrayal, adventure and a happy ending! And we all *have* a story – our own story. Some parts are better than others and some we prefer not to remember, but they make up who we are and the role we play in God's story.

Sometimes, however, connecting with God is a story all by itself. How do you make that connection? What *is* God's story? Do you know how much God loves you? Do you know the authority God has given you? What do you expect from God? Do you understand what God expects from you? Have you asked him? Do you know how to say, "Hello!"? Do you know what to say after you say, "Hello!"?

I grew up on a farm. My life as a child was an isolated one. My mother and father both worked full time and I spent most summer days by myself. Mother always insisted on regular church attendance, for which I'll be eternally grateful! I enjoyed sitting with my cousins each week on the front pew [*hard* wooden bench]. There was a lot of talk about God and this picture of Jesus hanging over the altar – what was that all about? And who took his picture? Why did we spend time every week memorizing Bible scriptures and listening to stories about Jesus? Were they just great stories about a man who lived a long time ago, or was there more?

I was 8 years old when I met my hero, who subsequently became my lover and best friend! As the warm rain sprinkled down, I was sitting in the garden under an umbrella in a pink terrycloth bathing suit, surrounded by yellow pear tomatoes - salt shaker in hand. The rolling hills were beautiful! The leaves on the trees fell off during winter, but now they were back, green as ever. The grass had been brown all winter, but not anymore. The water lilies floated in the pond and the marigolds stood tall in the rich, garden soil. The calves were romping around the barnyard close to their mothers.

What did all this mean? I had never seen water lilies in the garden, or marigolds in the pond. The mother cows never had little lambs; they always had bouncy little calves.

Could all of this be coincidence? Could it be magic? As I looked up in the sky, I considered if perhaps, just perhaps, this God or Jesus was really in control.

The clouds were fluffy and scattered, concealing the sun. I stared into the heavens, looking for some speck of something that might be looking back at me. *"Are you really there?"* My heart felt a familiar warmth. *"If you are really God or Jesus and you really control all these trees and grass and animals, then you could just give me a sign and I'll trust you and we'll be friends forever."*

I looked at my watch – 11:45. *"If you're really there, then just make my watch stop at 12:00 and I'll know you are real and want to be my friend."* It didn't seem to be such a hard thing to do *if*, in fact, he was in charge of all I had seen. Then I focused on other perplexing problems I'd encountered with people and questions wondering why things were the way they were.

Later that afternoon, forgetting the previous "deal" I offered God, I passed through the kitchen and saw the clock. It was 3:00. My heart began to race, my stomach tightened and my palms began to sweat. Did I dare look at my watch? What if it said 3:00? I would be so disappointed. What if it didn't? I turned my wrist and looked. It was 12:00 straight up! An overwhelming flood of confusion, joy and tears welled up inside as my entire body experienced the rush of a tingly covering. Shaking with fear, I felt I'd been dropped into an ongoing story and didn't have the slightest clue what I was supposed to do now. I did know one thing - a new relationship had just begun. I found treasure far greater than I had ever imagined!

A creator, a father, a king, a judge, a controller, a lawgiver, a friend to a lonely little eight year-old girl in a garden! Who ever would have thought that a God who was so busy running the world would have time to personally connect with me – a nobody? What an awesome God!

I needed to tell someone…. but who, and *what*? I ran through several scenarios and finally decided I'd be better off just keeping our relationship a secret. Frankly, I loved the idea of having a secret friend. It was a warm, tender relationship and I adored Him, whoever He was. I had plenty of questions. I started paying much closer attention at church and asking about things that were on my mind. I discovered most people knew there was a God. They believed in God. They believed in Jesus. They believed that Jesus was the Son of God. They did *not*, however, believe he was capable of interacting with people the way He did with me.

There were definite periods of testing and uncertainty for about 13 years – not about our relationship, but about my role in our relationship. I finally grabbed my Bible and searched desperately for further direction. There had to be more, and there was. I found romance and adventure and battles and betrayals and promises and love. My journey, my walk with God, transformed my aloneness and insecurity into confidence and peace. And it all started the day I questioned God, and kept on questioning everything.

God has a plan for you and in order for you to understand that plan, you need to talk to him; discuss it with him. We call it prayer. It's the privilege of combining and developing your thoughts and feelings into a powerful conversation with God, whose Hebrew name is YHVH. He is the only living God, the one who gave you life and the ability to reflect the awesome, powerful image in which you were created!

Are you interested? If so, let's begin with just a bit of history. This earth has been here for thousands of years. How many thousands? That's asking for an argument. Some scientists swear the earth is billions of years old. Others, after tracking beach erosion just over the last two hundred years, tell us the earth cannot be over 10,000 years old or Indiana would be beach front property. Remember when we landed on the moon? The Apollo mission capsule had really long legs. Why? Scientists knew that if the earth was billions of years old there would be a severe accumulation of dust on the moon. Instead, there were only a few inches.

I don't know how long this earth has been here, but just in my lifetime technology has come a long way. Only 40 years ago, "high tech" would have meant having a Princess phone or a dishwasher or a color TV. Ok, so maybe you've never heard of a Princess phone. Just type three words in your search engine, "history princess phone" and you'll find these phones were a huge hit. They came out in 1959 and were wonderful because you could touch a button instead of using a rotary dial. We still had party lines *(shared a phone line with 3-4 other families)* but the touch tone phones were much better than the rotary dial phones and far more advanced than the first phone at our house, which was one you had to crank and ask the operator to connect you to Aunt Frances or Grandma *(and she knew them both)*!

Think of the advances in "technology" over the years – 500 years ago, 1,000 years ago, 2,000 years ago, and even 5,000 years ago. It is amazing how far we've come!

But where was God in all these inventions over the years? Front and center! He has been inspiring men and women to step up to the technology plate for thousands of years. Each new invention picks up data from past inventions to use for future inventions. He's the invisible coach putting his team together. He has guided us into an incredible new era, but instead of giving him praise, we've chosen to focus totally on man's ability.

In the mid to late 60's there was a lot of chatter questioning whether or not God was dead. A huge movement began to "remove" God from schools, homes, businesses and, sometimes, churches. The Blue Law was repealed, which was a law that originated in New England designed to regulate commercial business on Sundays. The purpose of this law was to enforce moral standards and prohibit specific forms of entertainment or recreation. Until the repeal, it was actually illegal to shop, or even write a check, on Sundays. Yes, beloved, we decided it was more important to do what *we* wanted to do on Sundays than what *God* wanted us to do.

This is actually the law we repealed.	*"If you keep your feet from breaking the Sabbath and from doing as you please on my holy day, if you call the Sabbath a delight and the* Lord's *holy day honorable, and if you honor it by not going your own way and not doing as you please or speaking idle words, then you will find your joy in the* Lord, *and I will cause you to ride upon the high places of the earth, and feed you with the heritage of Jacob your father, for the mouth of the* Lord *hath spoken it."* Isaiah 58:13-14 NIV

God's spirit is continually moving. People grow and change each day. Children learn new technology everyday. We're quite a moving target! The stuff we most often long for, search for, and work for is material. It's here for a short time and then wears out or breaks or rusts. If we can visualize ourselves as spiritual people in physical bodies, we begin to thirst for meaning, truth, and the ability to connect with God on solid ground.

My grandmother told me her first home in America was a log cabin in the woods and she had to walk about a mile to the creek to get water for cooking, baths, cleaning, etc. She patted my knee and in her very German dialect said, *"..and in the winter I had to break the ice with an ax!"* She dreamed of learning about computers, but spent time reading her Bible every afternoon while I took my nap.

We've gained a lot of speed, expertise, solutions, resolutions, and access to tremendous global knowledge; but not necessarily a lot of wisdom, truth *or* respect for one another. We have the ability to produce more with one compact personal computer, or cell phone, than a large room full of people could produce just a few years ago. We have the ability to save huge amounts of time and solve global problems. But instead of using these tools to make us better people – better neighbors, better friends and enriched families – we're stressed physically, emotionally, mentally and spiritually just trying to keep up.

Deep inside, there's this monumental void in our souls that keeps crying, "There's more, there's more" and all we seem to hear is "Do more, do more!" Technology provides great tools. We just need a healthy balance!

"My soul desires you in the night; yes, with my spirit within me will I seek you early: for when your judgments are in the earth, the inhabitants of the world will learn righteousness." **Isaiah 26:9 NKJV**	**Training 101**

There's a greater story going on than we're paying attention to. We've lost sight of God's story and, because we've lost his story, we're losing sight of *our* story. God provides incredible insight into living prosperous, healthy, powerful lives. We've just been too busy to listen. God's story is full of love and passion, danger and evil, romance, adventure, battles, heroes, villains, overcoming insurmountable odds, sacrifice *and* promise with a happy ending.

Is *your* life full of real adventure, fortune, romance, intrigue and purpose? Hollywood can bring it right into your living room in full character!

When life hurts, all too often we cling to Hollywood's story and make it our own. We take on the 'hero' roles and the 'savior' roles and the 'damsel in distress-please rescue me' roles. We become the characters, forgetting they're just actors. We want to be loved. We want the happy ending. We want to be powerful and feel good, but all too often we just end up couch potatoes addicted to soap operas.

We don't know God's story; it isn't in our hearts. Instead of embracing God's words with love and obedience, we're often empty and unhappy without true purpose, so we look to Hollywood to provide a great story for us.

We want a "happily ever after" ending, but how easy is that when mom and dad get a divorce, or there's a diagnosis of cancer, or a lost job, or drug addiction, or alcoholism, or death, or bankruptcy, or arrest? We're losing our hope, our story.

Beware	*"The thief [the evil one] comes for one reason only – to kill, to steal and to destroy. But I [Jesus] am come that you might have life and have it more abundantly!"* *John 10:10 NIV*

Things are not what they seem to be! Looking at the physical world, we're totally wrapped up trying to survive and find happiness or success; but all the while, the evil one is at work using every angle to destroy us and our families.

When you were born, the world didn't start all over again. You dropped into a particular community in a particular country in a particular situation with parents from different backgrounds. So how can you know what's been going on? How do you get the whole story?

How do you emerge victorious? How do you become a powerful, effective human being with a heart for God?

In effect, you've just walked into a room and heard, *"And by the way,"* the blonde added, *"that's not a Porsche, it's a Ferrari."* to which everyone is laughing hysterically. You have no idea what's funny and no one takes time to tell you the story. It's not funny to you, which sets you on edge. You feel left out, unhappy, disconnected, lonely, frustrated and upset.

In the same way, when you were born, your life, or your story, just dropped into an ongoing story that God began thousands of years ago and you are, in effect, having trouble fitting in - laughing and feeling connected - without knowing the rest of the story.

Your challenge is to find the rest of the story and reflect the powerful image you've been created in, rather than mimicking someone else's story. When you understand his story and his passion for a relationship with you, you'll begin to envision your role, your purpose and the authority he has given you to fully walk with him.

You might think the world is all about technology, fashion, money and possessions, but in reality, there is a journey you must take that started long ago. A huge spiritual battle is taking place and you have a warrior's role to learn and fulfill.

To be victorious in this battle, your story needs to be wrapped up in God's story like a State Fair corn dog. You know they drop that hot dog right smack dab into the middle of the corn batter and cover it all up! Then they bake it or fry it and you can't even tell if there's anything inside. It's like that with God. The whole point in life is to be so covered up in His batter that you can't see yourself. You stay safe and warm and are protected from the evil one, armed with the defense God's provided.

I've spent many years sorting through God's Word, and although I don't have all the answers by any means, hopefully I can shed some light on your story so you'll be able to spend more time in the action, hero and romance part, and less time spinning your wheels in the mud, or watching TV. If I had known *"the rest of the story"* years ago, my life would have been powerfully and totally different. No one told me I was created in the image of God or explained what that meant. Perhaps they didn't know either.

I've made many, many mistakes in life; lots of failures and disappointments – *and* discovered God still pursuing me every moment of every day. Now, let me be very clear! You *will* make mistakes and feel like a failure and be very disappointed many times. Do not be discouraged, though! These are growing lessons. All God's mighty men and women of the Bible experienced these lessons and you will be no different. The object is to listen and learn the first or second time, instead of struggling through the rest of your life trying to understand the first lesson!

"The Lord *himself goes before you and will be with you; he will never leave you nor forsake you. Do not be afraid; do not be discouraged."* *Deuteronomy 31:8 NIV*	**DO NOT** **BE** **DISCOURAGED!**

Ok, let's see if the story makes more sense now. *"A blonde, wanting to earn some money, decided to hire herself out as a handyman-type and started canvassing a wealthy neighborhood. She went to the front door of the first house and asked the owner if he had any jobs for her to do. 'Well, you can paint my porch. How much will you charge?' The blonde said, 'How about 50 dollars?' The man agreed and told her that the paint and ladders that she might need were in the garage. The man's wife, inside the house, heard the conversation and said to her husband, 'Does she realize that the porch goes all the way around the house?' The man replied, 'She should. She was standing right there on it.' A short time later, the blonde came to the door to collect her money. 'You're finished already?' he asked. 'Yes,' the blonde answered, 'and I had paint left over, so I gave it two coats.' Impressed, the man reached in his pocket for the $50. 'And by the way,' the blonde added, 'that's not a Porsche, it's a Ferrari.'"*

Knowing what went on before not only adds meaning, it completes the circuit. You now know what's funny and why. You feel good and connected and completed and can laugh.

And so it is with God's story. You will have many blonde moments in life. There will also be many times you'll be doing all the right things and still feel like you're stuck in the mud. God is working.

About the mud....

> *"Count it all joy when you fall into various trials, knowing this – that the testing of your faith works patience." James 1:2-3 AKJV*

About the mud. It's important to spend some time stuck in the mud. Growing up I loved to go barefoot in the mud puddles after a warm summer rain. Therapy for a happy heart – until I decided to cut across a newly plowed field after a rain (didn't want to take the long road around)! I had on knee-high boots, but soon found myself stuck so deep the mud was globbing in over the top. No one knew I was out there. No one could hear me but God, and my energy was quickly zapped just trying to pull one leg out of the mud and put it in front of the other one without falling down. That field grew about 10 miles that day and with every step, I was making another deal with God through my tears. We had a *long* talk that day.

> *"If anyone lacks wisdom, ask God, who gives to all men liberally and without reproach, and it will be given to him." James 1:5 NKJV*

Wisdom

The next time the field was wet, I took the longer road around, knowing it would actually take less time. But more importantly, I learned a lot about God, wisdom – and mud - that day. He let me choose which way to go and never left me alone. When I realized how much mud I was in, I also knew He was all I had. And when you get stuck in the mud, God will *not* leave you alone and He *will* be all you need. Just ask!

Make it simple.

> *"Father, HELP!*
> *I'm stuck in the mud. I made a bad choice. Please hold my hand and help me get home safely!"*

God has never tried to make life difficult. That was all my own doing – He let me make up my own mind and decide all by myself. He provided an instruction manual; I just hadn't read it yet. The problem is that wisdom, or good judgment, usually comes from a lot of bad judgment, or mistakes. In order to become wise, it is very important that we make a lot of mistakes – just not serious ones. So the goal is to choose your mistakes well, learn from them, and never let go of God's hand or his word!

"When you walk through deep waters, I will be with you; *and through the rivers, they shall not overflow you;* *when you walk through the fire, you will not be burned,* *nor shall the flame scorch you." Isaiah 43:2 NKJV*	**His promise!**

God's story is simple. He loves you passionately more every day. He is pursuing you and with good reason. He bought you and you belong to him. But here the story begins to get a little risky. You can ask for forgiveness and love him in return, or you can turn your back on him and embrace the world – you know, just stay too busy to spend time alone with him or listen to him. He will love you either way, but if you choose to love him, in return he'll adopt you personally and you'll inherit all rights to his kingdom – both now and forever.

If you turn from him and embrace the world.... Well, we'll get back to that part later.

<u>The rules are simple:</u>

1. **Walk with God**
2. **Fall Down**
3. **Get Up**
4. **Walk with God**
5. **Fall Down**
6. **Get Up**
7. **Walk with God**
8. **Fall Down**
9. **Get Up**
10. **Walk with God**

*"He has shown you what is good; and what does YHVH require of you, but to do justly, and to love mercy, and to **walk humbly with your God?**" Micah 6:8 NKJV*

*"**Though he fall**, he shall not be utterly cast down; for the L*ORD* upholds him with his hand." Psalm 37:24 AKJV*

*"Those who wait on the L*ORD* shall renew their strength; **they shall mount up** with wings like eagles, they shall run and not be weary, they shall walk and not faint."*

Isaiah 40:31 AKJV

The key is to always grab God's hand when you fall and ask Him to help you back up. I remember when my children took their first baby steps. I didn't expect them to take off running around the block - I knew they were going to fall. I took special precautions and tried to keep them from falling – or at least provide a soft landing, but I failed miserably. They fell many times when I wasn't there to help them up. But God will never fail you. I failed, but God cannot fail and cannot fall. Hold onto his hand tightly!

Hold on!	*"Though I walk into the middle of trouble, you will revive me; you will stretch out your hand against the wrath of my enemies and your right hand will save me." Ps 138:7 NKJV*

Know who he is and know the image in which you were created. Know the plans he has for you and walk in them. Fulfill the course. But how, ?, you say?

"Call me, and I will answer you, and show you great

and mighty things, which you do not know."

Jeremiah 33:3 NKJV

Call Him!

Be His friend.

Thoughts:

- Are you only driven to prayer when you've exhausted every other alternative? What message does that communicate to God?

- Are your prayers "one-way" in that you receive from God, but give him nothing?

- What about your story? Who are you and what is your purpose? What meaning and impact do you have on this world?

- How important are you in God's story?

- When things are going well, what is your relationship with God?

- Do you find yourself turning on the TV more often than opening your Bible? Why?

- Often our failures are far more important than our successes. Think about a time when you failed. How did you feel? What did you learn? How did it impact your relationship with God?

- Fifty years ago it was easy to find quiet time. We still have 24 hours in a day, 7 days in a week. Are we just "*busy*" or are we "*fruitful*" in God's eyes?

God's Story

To "pray" literally means, to *ask*, or to *plead*. Several years ago, while listening to a "corporate" prayer at a political function, I began to smile to myself and then silently asked God if he was listening. The prayer went something like this, *"Most Holy Father, we come before you today. We pray for our brothers and sisters. LORD, we pray for our troops in battle. We pray for those men and women at home – the families of our troops. We pray God's direction upon our lives if it be thy will. Look upon us with your love. Oh LORD, hear our prayer. Amen"*

We've all heard, and sometimes prayed, prayers like this one. But suddenly, putting myself in God's shoes, a bit of humor peeked out. In effect, the prayer could be interpreted like this, *"Most Holy Father, we come before you today. We ask for our brothers and sisters. LORD, we ask for our troops in battle. We ask for those men and women at home – the families of our troops. We ask God's direction upon our lives unless you want us to follow someone else. Look at us, LORD. Oh LORD, listen to us. Amen"*

Can you imagine the look on God's face as he listens to us? As we build a close relationship with God, it's critical to listen to what we say to him. The first sentence lifts God in praise – and that's good. The next three sentences begin to ask for something, but 'what' isn't clearly defined. The only actual request is for God's direction, *maybe*, and for him to look at them and hear the prayer.

Even while I chuckled silently, God, in his love and grace, knew the intent of the heart. It was a privilege to feel his warm smile, like a parent encouraging his child's achievement. Prayer is the utmost achievement for a child of God. YHVH is a great teacher – we're just distracted students!

In addition, learning to pray, understanding the battle *(or training to fight it)*, hasn't been a priority. We're all busy with jobs and schedules and people and responsibilities. Satan knows if we're busy enough, we won't have any time for God. Without time for God, he can't train us. Without proper training, we won't know what God expects us to do, or how to do it. We won't understand the strategy against the enemy. Our prayers, while full of good intention, will profit us nothing.

19

"Even when you do ask, you don't get it because you ask amiss...."
James 4:3 KJV

I grew up in a quaint little country church. Outside of memorizing the 23rd Psalm we focused on the New Testament. Don't get me wrong, there's great stuff going on in the New Testament! But as I searched to understand God's heart, I was drawn to the Old Testament where I discovered God's passion and sovereignty. I fell in love with YHVH in the book of Isaiah.

While my children were growing up, many nights before bedtime I would read to them from God's word, except that I created the "Mama Reagan" version from King James since it was my only Bible. To this day, sometimes I have to check to see which version I'm in, so please read along in your Bible as we pass scriptures – particularly if they're unfamiliar to you. Please allow me to share some incredible discoveries and insights as we look into this remarkable story – God's 'boot camp' version.

♥ ♥ ♥

Once upon a time, a long time ago in a far away place called Eden, God's story began where the Euphrates River meets the Tigris River. Today we call it Iraq.

From the beginning (Genesis 1:1) God had a plan. He created many galaxies throughout the universe, and everything within them - earth, atoms, animals, microbes, seeds, plants, DNA, rocks, mountains, trees, rivers, etc. - all in six days, but not in just *any* random order. He's a fabulous planner and designer!

In the first chapter of Genesis we're told the earth had no form – there was just a void with darkness – and the Spirit of God moved upon the face of the waters. But watch what happened next!

God *spoke* words and things appeared. ___He said___:

Day 1 "Let there be light" – and daylight and darkness appeared. The evening and morning were the first day - 24 hours.	**Day 4** "Let there be lights in the sky" – and the sun, moon and stars appeared to divide day from night; for signs; for seasons; and for days and years.
Day 2 "Let there be sky" (a space) between the waters above and the waters below – and it appeared.	**Day 5** "Let there be creatures and animals" to fill the waters and the sky – and they appeared.
Day 3 Let the "waters" under the sky gather in one place and let the "dry land" appear with vegetables and herbs and all kinds of seeds.	**Day 6** "Let there be living creatures and beasts" to fill the earth – and they appeared. "Let us create man in our image."

Notice the alignment of the days of creation. God did not create man or stars before he created a place to put them. The first three days he set the stage: daylight and darkness; sky separating the waters; and then land. The next three days he filled the stage in the same sequence. The sun, stars and moon were spoken into being on the fourth day, to complement the daylight and darkness. The winged creatures and sea creatures were created the fifth day to fill the sky and the waters already created on the second day. On the sixth day, when God created man and the animals to roam the earth, there were herbs and vegetables for them to eat, already created on the third day. Everything was planned and created in order.

ORDER	*"Let all things be done decently and in order."* *1 Corinthians 14:40 NKJV*

Genesis provides the short version of what happened each creation day, however, further insight into creation details are found throughout the Bible. Proverbs 8:29 describes God's orders to the waters, that they should not pass his commandment. In Job 26:10 KJ21 we find the length of time they are to obey - *"He compassed the waters with a boundary, until the day and night come to an end."* In Job 9 we find God also gave commands to the sun and the star constellations Arcturus,

21

Orion and Pleiades. Then in Job 26:7 AKJV, relative to the earth, *"He stretches out the north over the empty place and hangs the earth upon nothing."*

God commanded his creation into place. Did creation obey his commands? Are the sun and stars still shining and is the earth still hanging on nothing? The disciples were astonished when Jesus rebuked the wind and the sea in Mark 4:39. They looked at each other in amazement that the wind and the sea obeyed him! In Ezekiel 36:6-8, we find God actually apologizing to the mountains, to the hills, to the rivers and to the valleys because they bore the shame of the bloodshed of the nations. *What a God!*

And yet man, whom God loves with a fervent passion, was created with the freedom to make his own choices, including obedience to God. Why? Because there is no glory in a relationship without choice. God is most glorified when he's glorified in us! When God truly satisfies your every need, you are whole, and God is glorified!

Everything that was created the first six days came from nothing. Absolutely nothing! But by the power of God's words, incredible life and order appeared. Could he have created it all in a different order? Sure. So why did he choose this order?

From the very beginning (Genesis 1:1), God is teaching us by example. But is God teaching physical lessons or spiritual lessons?

If we want an abundant garden, we plant according to his example. First we prepare the soil with all the right nutrients to encourage good growth. Then we plant seeds *which must die* before they can grow and nourish our physical bodies. (You missed that on your last trip to the supermarket, didn't you?) ☺

Now turn to Matthew 13:3. Jesus is trying to teach his closest friends because they're not getting it. Interestingly enough he's using the same method of teaching as God did in Genesis 1 - words and seeds and getting the ground prepared. But Jesus mingles this physical word-seed stuff with spiritual implications. It is the parable of a man planting seeds.

Seeds self-perpetuate in obedience to God's command (*Day 3*) from generation to generation, but great things happen when care is taken to plant them properly. The purpose of the parable is to explain what happens to seeds, and compares seeds being planted in prepared soil to God's word being planted in prepared hearts.

Placement of Seeds/Words	Matthew 13:3-23		
	Physical Application	**Spiritual Application**	**Example**
Wayside	You're planting seeds and on the way to the garden some fall to the wayside and get picked off by the birds.	Your ears hear the word of God, but before you can understand it, it's picked off by the wicked one.	You read the Bible, but don't understand it. You get frustrated and confused, decide it's not worth it, and go back to your old habits.
Rocks & Stones	You're planting seeds and on the way to the garden some fall on the rocks.	Your ears hear the word of God, but your spiritual roots aren't deep and when you try to understand, you're offended and give up easily.	You read the Bible, and get really excited, but when sickness or sorrow or hardship come, you become disillusioned, not knowing it's part of God's plan.
Thorns	You're planting seeds and on the way to the garden some fall in the thorns.	Your ears hear the word of God, but before you can plant it in your heart and establish roots, or blessings, you get too busy focusing on problems and daily demands, and the world chokes it out.	You read your Bible and attend church regularly, but then take on too many outside duties, or focus on the things of others, and decide you don't have time and become unfruitful.
Prepared Dirt	You're planting seeds in the rich garden soil, faithfully watering and applying great fertilizer.	Your ears hear the word of God; you firmly plant it in your heart daily, establish blessings, and walk with God.	You read the Bible, study it daily, memorize it, seek God's will and share it with others. Through all your trials you trust God.

Jesus is teaching us how to have a relationship with God. Suddenly, God's words and the seeds and the prepared ground have new meaning. The disciples knew dirt. They knew seeds. They didn't understand how to walk with God. Jesus pulls together what they knew with what they didn't know, through their physical ears and their hearts, and then gently explains the spiritual meaning.

Like seeds, God's *words* also self-perpetuate in obedience to God's command from generation to generation, and great things happen when we take care to explain them to our children from generation to generation.

SEEDS **&** **WORDS**	*"…as the rain comes down and the snow falls from heaven, it does not return there, but waters the earth and makes it bring forth and bud that it may give seed to the sower and bread to the eater. So shall my word be that goes forth out of my mouth; it shall not return unto me void, but it shall accomplish that which I please, and it shall prosper in the thing I've sent it to." Isaiah 55:10-11 NKJV* *"… Man does not live by bread only, but by every word that proceeds out of the mouth of the LORD does man live." Deut 8:3b NKJV*

As we focus on prayer, remember God's promise. His word will accomplish whatever pleases him and it shall prosper wherever it's sent. God commands "*his word*" is to be the main source of our lives – the main seed from which we grow.

He was clothed with a robe dipped in blood, and His name is called The Word of God. *Revelation 19:13 NASB*	**WORD OF** **GOD**

From the beginning, God has a plan for you. He will help you prepare the soil of your heart to receive him. And if your seed is willing to die to self-centered things, grab his word, hide it in your heart daily, and reflect his image, then he will lead you, protect you, bless you and cause you to ride upon the high places of the earth.

On our most intelligent days, we grasp only a small fragment of who God is and rarely ponder the power he's extended to us. We have *no* idea where he came from or why he loves us so passionately. And yet, he loves us so much he gave us the inherent ability to build a powerful relationship with him and to reflect his image - the image in which we were created.

Ponder Your Power!	*"Let us create man in our image..."* *Genesis 1:26 AKJV*

Within verse 26 of the first chapter of Genesis, YHVH says, *"Let us make man in our image...."* Hhmm. A couple things come to mind. First of all, who is "us" and what is the image of "us"? You have been given power to reflect the image in which you were created! Wouldn't you like to understand your purpose – and in whose image you were created?

Image! What is an image? Have you ever looked into a quiet pond, or a mirror? What you see is a reflection of you. It's your image. It's not you, but it *looks like* you. You have *not* been given the power to become a god, but you *have* been given the privilege to reflect the powerful image of the Almighty, Living God!

From Genesis we know YHVH is the one who spoke creation into being. But let's look at who else was with YHVH in the beginning when he created the heavens and the earth.

INHERITENCE POWER   IMAGE, OR REFLECTION

YHVH

"In the beginning, God created the heavens and the earth."

Genesis 1: 1 NASB

".. put on the new man, which is renewed in knowledge after the image of him that created him."

Colossians 3:10 KJV

SPIRIT of YHVH

"And the Spirit of God moved upon [shattered] the face of the waters."

Genesis 1:2b AKJV

"But you will receive power when the Holy Spirit comes on you; and you will be my witnesses in Jerusalem, and in all Judea and Samaria, and to the ends of the earth."

Acts 1:8 NIV

WORD / JESUS

"In the beginning was the Word, and the Word was <u>with</u> God, and the Word <u>was</u> God. ....And the Word was <u>made flesh</u> and <u>dwelt among us</u>."

John 1:1,14 AKJV

"Through faith we understand that the worlds were framed by the word of YHVH [Jesus] so that things that are seen were not made out of things that appear."

Hebrews 11:3 AKJV

WISDOM

"The Lord possessed me [Wisdom] in the beginning of his way, before his works of old. I was set up from everlasting from the beginning, or ever the earth was. Before mountains were settled, before the hills, while as yet he had not made the earth, nor the fields.... When he prepared the heavens, I was there."

Proverbs 8:22,23,25a,26a,27a KJV

"Happy is the man that finds wisdom and gets understanding. It's better than silver or gold, more precious than rubies, and nothing can be compared to her. Length of days are in her right hand and in her left hand riches and honor. Her ways are ways of pleasantness, and all her paths are peace. She is a tree of life to those who lay hold upon her, and happy is everyone that retains her."

Proverbs 3:14-18 MRV

Now it makes more sense when God said, "Let <u>us</u> create man in <u>our</u> image." You are created in the image of:

- God, whose name is **YHVH**

- The **Spirit of God**, or the Holy Spirit

- The **Word** of God, with incredible power to create something out of nothing

- **Jesus**, the Son of God, the Word, and the only living way to eternity with God

- **Wisdom**.

From what we know of the first four – God, the Holy Spirit, the Word and Jesus– they are one. This is confusing because we're humans, not gods, and we weren't given details.

Perhaps this analogy will help. Water is technically two parts hydrogen and one part oxygen. It is written H_2O. However, it comes in three forms: solid, liquid and vapor. If you take a piece of ice and drop it into a pan of boiling water, at least temporarily you have all three forms. <u>Ice</u> is hard and cold, <u>steam</u> is vapor and hot, and <u>water</u> is liquid and can be warm, cold or hot. We call them ice, steam, and water. But they are all forms of water; they are all H_2O.

If we still don't totally understand how God, Jesus, the Word, and the Holy Spirit are one, and we don't, we *are* given great insight into their powerful connection.

And then there is Wisdom. She teaches great and mighty things and we need to make every effort to attain her.

WISDOM	*"..Wisdom is better than rubies; and all the things that may be desired are not to be compared to it."* *Prov. 8:11 AKJV*

Now we know with whom God was speaking in Genesis 1:26. There may have been others present, but the only ones mentioned are God, the Holy Spirit, Jesus, the Word, and Wisdom.

If you have been created in the image of all of these, where is your strength? What power have you inherited? What is your image?

Just in the *first* chapter of Genesis we get a glimpse of God's abilities. He's a planner, a fabulous designer. He's organized. He's able to distinguish between good and evil; he has great knowledge and the power to make things happen when his words are spoken. He loves his people and is a "giver." He gave us all we have and all we are, and in return only asks for *our* love. <u>We</u> were created in this image.

And, like you and me, Adam and Eve were created in the image of God. He placed them in a beautiful garden called Eden and told them they could eat from all of the trees except the Tree of Knowledge of Good and Evil.

"Oh, that there were such a heart in them, that they would fear me, and keep all my commandments always, that it might be well with them and with their children forever!" *Deuteronomy 5:29 KJV*	**GOD'S DESIRE**

Unfortunately, reading through the next couple chapters of Genesis, neither Adam nor Eve was honest with God. In the beginning, God turned over his authority to Adam and Eve. However, through sin and disobedience, Adam and Eve actually turned God's authority over to Satan, God's enemy!

When God confronted them *(after having eaten the fruit he told them not to)* there was no repentance, only blame. Adam blamed Eve and also implied it was really God's fault [*that woman <u>you</u> gave me, she gave it to me*] and, of course, Eve blamed the serpent.

But what about repentance? Did either Adam or Eve ever say, "Father, I'm so very sorry. Won't you please forgive me?"

God punished Adam and Eve for their disobedience and then (*I love this*) he made clothes for them (Genesis 3:21) before he threw them out of the garden. A disappointed father disciplined his children for being disobedient and then lovingly made clothes for them. Shouldn't we all reflect this image?

Further, we find that Cain reflected the same attitude as his parents when God approached him about his offering and the whereabouts of his brother, Abel.

In Genesis 4:3-4, both Cain and Abel brought offerings to God. Did you ever wonder why? Did they make this up? No. God instructed them both in the process of offerings. If not, why would Abel think it would be cool to kill a beautiful, pure and spotless young lamb and offer it to God with the fat? *YUCK!* Yet his offering had God's respect. Then we're told neither Cain, *nor his offering*, received God's respect.

Within the first seven chapters of Leviticus great details of acceptable sacrifices are revealed with specific instructions including lambs and the fat, as well as special instructions for offerings of first fruits, so we know God taught both Cain and Abel appropriate sacrifices and offerings.

God, however, knew Cain's heart. God asked Cain why he was angry, and then he asked Cain why, if he'd done his best and tried his hardest, wouldn't his offering be acceptable? *'But if not, sin is crouching at your door and while his desire is to consume you, you have the power to rule over him.'* This verse from Genesis 4:7 is the *"Mama Reagan"* version. Please read it in your Bible and hover over it awhile.

God is confirming to Cain the image he was created in and the power he'd inherited to overcome the evil one. Wow! God is trying to mentor Cain and lead him to victory. Cain's sinful heart *(perhaps his attitude)* brought God no respect, *as well as* Cain's offering. What if Cain had swallowed his pride, repented of his sin, and asked God's forgiveness along with specific directions on how to overcome this evil one?

The battle for Cain's heart had begun.

<table>
<tr><td>YHVH</td><td>"I have appeared to you … to open their eyes, and to turn them from darkness to light, and from the power of Satan unto God, that they may receive forgiveness of sins, and inheritance among them which are sanctified by faith that is in me."
Acts 26:16a,18 AKJV</td></tr>
</table>

Cain's response, like that of his mother and father, was full of attitude, not repentance. He killed his brother, and when God called him on it and asked where Abel was, he lied, said he didn't know, and claimed he wasn't his brother's keeper. And, like his mother and father, his punishment did not bring repentance, but only complaints that his punishment was more than he could bear. Genesis 4.

Here, within this story of two brothers, there is a subliminal message line which runs throughout God's story that mustn't be overlooked. Why did the sacrifice of the lamb gain God's respect? Was it because Abel's heart was right with God? Was it because Abel was obedient to God's command? Or was it because God is teaching us, from the beginning, about the coming sacrifice of the pure and spotless Lamb of God and how to prepare our hearts to walk with God in obedience?

There is another parallel story in Genesis 15 we cannot overlook. Abram is questioning God's gift of the land of Canaan as his inheritance since he has no children and isn't a young pup. Abram doesn't doubt God; but he's inquiring what this inheritance means to him without children. He does have servants and they have children, though. Is this God's intention?

God tells Abram to look at the stars in the sky and see if he can count them all. (*Obviously he can't.*) That's how many children Abram will have – too many to count! God reminds Abram how he called him out of Ur, the land of the Chaldeans, and brought him to this land. Abram's children will inherit it – not those of his servants.

So Abram asks how he's to know this will happen.

We begin to see the reason God calls Abraham "friend". God and Abram have a very close relationship. Abram has a question – he goes right to God with it. Doesn't matter if he doesn't understand or doesn't get it – he goes right to God with it. Unlike Cain, Abram is looking to God for wisdom and direction; for understanding and purpose in his life.

In Genesis 9:5-6 after the flood, God explains to Noah that God *will* require the blood of our lives, so before moving on, let's focus a moment on the term *"blood covenant,"* which is a contractual agreement of giving blood for blood.

In fact, the law requires that nearly everything be cleansed with blood, and without the shedding of blood there is no forgiveness.
Hebrews 9:22 NIV

FORGIVENESS CONTRACT

Blood covenant law was tradition. Each party of a blood covenant would sacrifice his own animal on opposite sloping grounds so the blood of each animal would flow down together into a mingled pool. Then each covenant party would remove his shoes and walk barefooted through the pool of mixed blood, promising to keep his word, his part of the covenant. If he did not keep his promise, it would cost him his own blood, his own life.

In Genesis 15, in response to Abram's question, God prepares a blood covenant with Abram. He instructs Abram to bring a heifer, a goat and a ram; to kill them and divide them in half on opposite slopes. He also asked for a dove and a pigeon to be sacrificed, but left whole. Then God placed Abram in a deep sleep while God took on both sides of the covenant, walking barefoot through this pool of mingled blood in the form of a blazing torch.

Why a blood covenant? Abram understood blood covenant. He knew the serious impact of this commitment. What did it mean? Under a normal blood covenant, both Abram and God would have walked barefoot through the mixed blood, each being responsible only for their covenant promise.

BUT GOD took on the promise and consequences of *both* sides of this blood covenant while Abram slept. Therefore, if God went back on his word and didn't keep his commitment to give the promised inheritance to Abram and his children forever and ever, then God would give his blood – his life. BUT ALSO if Abram or any of his heirs went back on their word and didn't keep *their* commitment to YHVH, God would give his life. If this covenant was broken by *either* party for *any* reason whatsoever – God's unfaithfulness or Abram's – God would pay the penalty. *He* would pay the price – his blood.

If the vision of the sacrifice of the Lamb of God wasn't apparent to us at Abel's offering, it's confirmed in Genesis, chapter 15. At this moment, God sealed his promise to come to earth as one of us in the form of Jesus Christ, the pure and holy spotless Lamb of God, to take on the burden of the cross not only to redeem us, pay for our sins, retrieve the authority Adam and Eve handed over to Satan and return it to us; but also because of a promise to his dear friend.

Now please catch this story line. Right before God drove Adam and Eve from Eden, there's another conversation among those in whose image we're created. It goes something like this in Genesis 3:22. *'Well, man has become one of us in the knowledge of good and evil. Now we have to make sure he doesn't get his hands on the Tree of Life or his fate will be sealed forever.'*

What in the world are they talking about?

One Paradise garden – Eden. Apparently *two* forbidden trees within the garden: the Tree of Knowledge of Good and Evil, and the Tree of Life. Being created with the freedom to make their own choices, once Adam and Eve discovered evil and transferred their God-given authority to Satan, if they were to eat of the Tree of Life, they would be sealed in their sins forever without opportunity for salvation from, or redemption of, their sins. Some type of remission for sins, some type of atonement, some type of payment must be made. Therefore, they must not be allowed to come close to the Tree of Life before God himself could atone for their sins.

Now before you think these were just fairy tale trees, turn to Revelation 22:1-2. After the tribulation, after the 1,000 year millennium, after the judgment, as we're walking with God in Paradise, here is the Tree of Life to *sustain* us throughout eternity! In Genesis 3:24 God set cherubim with a flaming sword to guard the Tree of Life. I have no idea where it is at this moment, but you may be assured it's in good hands. God *will* bring it back to Paradise at the appointed time.

God's story continues through testimonies of Abraham, Isaac, Israel, Joseph, and Moses. Then, while rescuing his people, the nation of Israel, through a series of marvelous miracles, YHVH initiated a series of seven Feasts Israel must obey, beginning with the first Passover as they leave Egypt. These Feasts have multiple purposes and provide awesome insight into YHVH's plan for all humanity as he continues to teach us. *(And yes, Jesus fulfills ALL the feasts! The Word, the Savior, that precious Lamb of God, Jesus!)*

As the nation of Israel followed God into and through the wilderness, the powerful witness of God's faithfulness should have been enough to encourage them to trust him with everything. For forty years their shoes didn't even wear out – no need for leather retreads! What a God!

Why did they wander around for 40 years? God wasn't lost. But the "old" generation of unbelievers *was lost* spiritually. God knew the Israelites would never make it on their own in the new land without him, and those coming out of Egypt had no spiritual commitment to God. They had become slaves, not only to the pharaoh, but also to sin. They had not passed down the seed of God's word from generation to generation as they were commanded by God to do. Therefore, they wandered about in the wilderness until all the "old" generation (anyone over 40 years old) died off. Only those born in freedom and trained under YHVH's personal protection in the wilderness would move into the Promised Land. God took his time to teach them the rewards of obedience and faith.

It's also important to understand that until Christ was born, ONLY bonafide Jews, sons of Abraham, Isaac and Israel, were God's children, and he was to be their *only* God.

YHVH instructed the Jews not to follow other gods; not to sacrifice their children; and not to intermarry with other people.

"Therefore, do not give your daughters in marriage to their sons or take their daughters for your sons. Do not seek a treaty of friendship with them at any time, that you may be strong and eat the good things of the land and leave it to your children as an everlasting inheritance."

> *Ezra 9:12 NIV*

BONAFIDE ISRAELITES

Upon entering the Promised Land, challenges abounded. The people wanted a king. God didn't want them to have a king. YHVH was their king. But the people insisted.[1] So YHVH provided judges and kings, many driven from their own human limitations, and they led God's nation into disobedience, idolatry and perversion. YHVH sent prophets to warn them of the resulting devastation to their moral and spiritual state, however, they chose not to listen and finally told YHVH to leave them alone, so he did – for four hundred forty-six years.

SILENCE

"Behold, the day is coming that I will send a famine in the land, not a famine of bread, nor a thirst for water, but of hearing the words of the LORD…" Amos 8:11 KJV

"They shall go with their flocks and with their herds to seek the LORD, but they shall not find him; he has withdrawn himself from them. " Hosea 5:6 AKJV

GONE!

And ***then*** YHVH fulfilled his covenant commitment to Abram.

---

[1] I Samuel 8:6-9; 12

Thoughts:

- God's passion for, and protection of, *his* people was perhaps clearest when God actually killed 185,000 Assyrians coming up against Jerusalem during King Hezekiah's reign. King Hezekiah was really nervous and so he took the threatening letter from King Sennacherib straight to God, laid it out before him and pleaded, through a marvelous prayer[2] for God to save them. The next morning it was reported that King Sennacherib's entire army of 185,000 men had been killed during the night by an angel sent by YHVH. How would history have changed if King Hezekiah had *not* prayed to God?

- *Your image* (the one you inherited at creation):

    Creative, Planner, Ability to Discern Good from Evil, Wisdom, Power, Holy, Organized, *"Empowered"* to Speak Life-Changing Words, Faithful, Loving, Trusting, Merciful, Gracious, Eternal, Accountable, Steadfast, Sincere, Committed, Passionate, Peaceful, Orderly, Fruitful, Forgiving, Obedient, Giver. These are attributes of God you have inherited. Which attributes do you think you fulfill? Which attributes would God say you fulfill?

"Plow up the hard ground of your hearts!
Do not waste your good seed among thorns.
Surrender your pride and power.
Change your hearts before the LORD,
or my anger will burn like an unquenchable fire
because of all your sins."

Jeremiah 4:3b, 4b NLT

---

[2] 2 Kings 19

Relationship

About your relationship with God.... What is the intent of your heart? Are you looking for a fulfilling relationship with a lifetime commitment or do you just want God to answer your prayers and then give you some space? We live in a microwave society and, quite frankly, we usually want what we want when we want it. Take a moment and ask yourself honestly what it is you want from God.

Prayer is your *relationship* application to the Almighty Creator of the heavens and earth. How would you describe your relationship with God? Is it strong and confident enough you can ask God for anything and expect to receive it? Or is the *only* time he hears from you when you want, or need, something?

This chapter will highlight some critical elements, or qualities, of relationship as they relate to prayer, and show how a balanced relationship with God will bring more power to your life *and* your prayers.

This intimate, personal relationship requires time to think, time to listen, and commitment to God. We *sort of* understand because we've developed strong relationships, friendships; we've fallen in love. We've had intimate, personal relationships with people.

At times, however, human relationships become a problem when the person we've trusted to be our best friend, or lover, or spouse, or child, or neighbor betrays us. And because Adam and Eve handed over their God-given authority to Satan, we also inherited Satan's authority to tempt us, which usually draws us in, hook, line and sinker. But God will never betray us. Therefore, we must not only trust him explicitly, but we must also strive to become the person he can trust.

Solid relationships have specific elements, or qualities, tied to the heart, such as honor, trust, commitment, respect, honesty, sincerity, accountability, grace, passion, etc. A balanced relationship is one where both parties extend the same elements of relationship equally to one another. And because these relationships are woven into, and throughout God's story, we'll begin there.

Before God fulfilled his commitment to Abram and came to earth in the form of a baby boy, God's *only* relationships were with his people: Abraham, Isaac, Jacob, and their descendents - the nation of Israel. He loved them, led them, provided for all their needs and protected them from other nations. He loved them as a groom loves his bride.

BRIDEGROOM	*God will rejoice over you as a bridegroom rejoices over his bride.* *Isaiah 62:5b AKJV*

A loving father – a faithful groom – YHVH knew the importance of love and obedience in a relationship. However, the Israelites didn't want to be obedient and eventually broke off their relationship with YHVH. Like Adam and Eve, they wanted God's blessing and protection, but not the responsibility of the relationship that goes with it.

"Does a bride hide her wedding dress? No! Yet for years on end my people have forgotten me." *Jeremiah 2:32b MRV*	**BRIDE**

All through the Old Testament God struggled to find people who would obey him; people who would put a relationship with him above everything else in life. Separation from Israel for 446 years broke his heart and moved him to write a new law; build a new relationship.

NEW

RELATIONSHIP

"For unto us a child is born, unto us a son is given, and the government will be on his shoulders. And he will be called Wonderful Counselor, Mighty God, Everlasting Father, Prince of Peace."

Isaiah 9:6 AKJV

This new law, this new relationship, would be offered not only to Israel but to all mankind. YHVH himself would come to earth personally in the form of a newborn baby to capture hearts. He would provide step-by-step training for his troops, guiding them every step of the way, rescuing them from the fall, building a firm foundation for all future generations to stand upon. He would fulfill all his promises, pour out all his love, and recruit eternal relationships with those who would honor and love him in return.

And once again, Israel rejected him.

The temple curtain sealing off the Holy of Holies (*the part of the temple where God lived*) ripped apart from top to bottom[3] as Christ died a torturous death on the cross. This curtain had separated the Israelites from God; only the high priest was allowed to enter into the Holy of Holies where God lived. But at the moment of his last breath on the cross, the curtain wall ripped down the middle, and access to the Most High God became up close and personal.

The new relationship had begun.

This new freedom, this new relationship, was very difficult for the Jews to understand. This was *not* the law they'd been taught. This was a new law.

"But Christ came as High Priest of the good things to come, with the greater and more perfect tabernacle not made with hands, that is, not of this creation. Not with the blood of goats and calves, but with His own blood He entered the Most Holy Place once for all, having obtained eternal redemption."

Hebrews 9:11–12 NKJV

THE NEW LAW

---

[3] Matthew 27:51

In the early 1980's I worked in a department store in Downtown Indianapolis. There were a lot of issues in my life and a fair amount of pressure, professionally and financially, and one particular day the pressure shoved my gears into overload. I didn't actually verbalize my displeasure, but you *could* say my heart wasn't aligned with God's Spirit. I kept internalizing 'stuff,' keeping it to myself all day, putting on a smile and a "sure, no problem" response, but deep inside I hurt.

Trudging out to the car at the end of the day, carrying the weight of the world on my shoulders *(and a lot of self pity)*, I got settled in and turned the key many times. Nothing happened. No noise. Not even a click. After an infuriating few minutes, tears began rolling down my cheeks as I held my face in my hands and poured out my heart to God.

"There's nothing wrong with this car, is there?" I sobbed. *(Silence)*

"This is about my attitude, isn't it?" *(More silence)*

"I am so sorry. I haven't been walking in your love, or trusting you. You have given me so much and I am so unworthy. Please forgive me!"

The weight of the world was immediately lifted off my shoulders and his familiar presence poured over me like a gentle, warm shower. After I wiped up all the water from my tears, I tried the key again. The car started right up – and I praised God for loving me when I was ugly, and for teaching me about his sovereignty.

Relationship is <u>critically</u> important to prayer!

Take a moment here. What was this all about? How did I *know* there was nothing wrong with my car? Because I knew my Father. This was one of those many times when he gave me a "time out" and, because there had been so many, I knew I could either sit there and sulk, or repair the attitude he depends upon in our relationship.

YHVH cared about me far above all the other stuff in my life, and believe me I didn't have a perfect life *(and still don't)*. I kept tripping up and falling into foxholes on the battle field. He kept extending his hand and waiting patiently for me to listen to his soft words.

"Come here, sweetheart. Just sit on my lap and let me hold you for a minute. I love you and want what's best for you. Take a couple deep breaths and relax. Now, listen to me."

Listen to me. He has NEVER criticized or condemned me. Sometimes it feels like the whole world has, but not God.

<table>
<tr><td>

TIME OUT

</td><td>

"He who spares his rod hates his son, but he who loves him disciplines him promptly."

Proverbs 13:24 NKJV

</td></tr>
</table>

Through my relationship with YHVH I have gained a tremendous acknowledgment of his power and awesome authority. Connecting with God and depending upon him daily develops faith. When you develop as much faith in God as you have in the chair in which you're sitting, you'll be able to move mountains. But faith comes through relationship, and relationship comes when you put on God's shoes, look through his eyes, and walk with him, hand-in-hand, while he reveals his story.

<table>
<tr><td>

"Even if you had faith as small as a mustard seed," the LORD answered, "you could say to this mulberry tree, 'May God uproot you and throw you into the sea,' and it would obey you!"

Luke 17:6 NASB

</td><td>

FAITH

</td></tr>
</table>

At the beginning of Jesus' ministry, Mark witnessed a woman who came to Jesus pleading for the healing of her daughter. She was Greek and her daughter had a 'not-so-nice' unclean spirit. Jesus simply told her that the Jews, God's children, must be taken care of first. He said it's not right to take bread away from God's children and throw it to the dogs.

But this Greek woman wasn't moved. She wanted Jesus' healing. She knew he could heal her daughter and she knew he was their only hope. She communicated her faith so clearly and powerfully that Jesus healed her daughter.

<table>
<tr>
<td>

DISCOVER YOUR POWER!

</td>
<td>

*"And she answered him, 'Yes, L*ORD*; yet the dogs under the table eat the children's crumbs.' And he said to her, 'For this saying [because you have asked with so much faith], go your way; the demon is gone out of your daughter.'"*

Mark 7:28-29 NKJV

</td>
</tr>
</table>

Be the Greek woman. Look at her prayer. That was an Abraham conversation, if you ask me! She had so much faith in Christ she wasn't about to be moved. She honored him as "LORD" even though he called her a dog. She hadn't studied in the Temple or gone to group meetings, but she knew the power of God when she saw it.

But what brought the healing into her daughter? Christ clearly stated it wouldn't be right to grant her request, and then actually referred to her as a dog. What changed his mind?

Again, God is teaching us. Her "words" moved Christ, who brought healing into her daughter. She had no power to heal, but she knew who did. She walked in the image of God, the image in which she was created. When God spoke words, creation appeared. When the Greek woman spoke words, her daughter was healed and the demon was gone.

What would have happened if she'd said, *"Oh, silly me. I guess you're right. Well, if you ever change your mind, or if it's somewhere in your will, would you think about healing my daughter?"*

Her ***words*** revealing her honor and trust in the power of Israel's God, a critical element of relationship, connected her to the ability to receive healing.

There is an incredible power each of us inherited from God. It is the power of the spoken word. Whether or not she knew God's story, she trusted in him and his sovereignty over evil. Through the power of God's image, she spoke her desire boldly, with faith and confidence, and God granted her wish. Our Father is like that. Yes, he is!

As children of God, we *should* reflect the image of our Father. Parents aren't usually surprised to hear comments that their children look like them *(and hopefully they're not disappointed when they act like them!)* Just like at home, reflecting our Father's image is far easier when we spend quality time with him, obey him, learn from him, understand his will, listen to his heart, and walk with him daily.

Throughout the Bible many ordinary people performed extraordinary feats – not because they had supernatural powers, but because they had a very close, personal, trusting relationship with God. They had a heart for God and they did what he told them to do. Abraham, Moses, Israel, Esther, Joseph, Daniel, David, Elijah and Hezekiah – to name just a few.

Did *they* reflect the image in which they were created? Some of them, yes; some of them, no. Even Jonah, who insisted on his own plans for awhile, came through and did exactly what God asked him to do, but did he ever realize the power of his image? Did he earnestly walk with God?

The closer you draw to God, the closer your personal relationship with him. The closer and deeper your personal relationship with God, the more you'll reflect his image. It just works that way.

God's plan for you is clearly defined. You are lost without him. You need a savior. He's recruiting warriors willing to study and work hard. Will you enlist? Are you willing to devote time to build a solid relationship with God?

If you're truly looking for an eternal relationship, starting right now, then how do you begin? How do you get close to God? If you feel a deep emptiness in your heart, a loneliness in your soul, or a desperate lack of purpose in your life, God is pursuing you!

What is your response? What does it mean to "know" God or "believe" in him? Can you know him or believe in him *without* having a personal relationship with him?

The demons know him and truly believe his power. So knowing and believing doesn't automatically make you a personal friend.

> "... [The demon said], 'Let us alone! ... Are you come to destroy us? I know you, I know who you are, the Holy One of God.'"
>
> *Mark 1:24a,c KJV*
>
> "You believe there is one God; that's good. The demons also believe and tremble." *James 2:19 KJ21*

> **Demons Know Jesus & Believe in Him!**

Jesus' brother, James, said that as you draw near to God, God will draw near to you. He also said we should wash our hands and clean up our heart. From James 4:8

Sounds like getting ready to eat, doesn't it? '*Go wash your hands and clean up for dinner!*' How many times have you heard that? So how does washing up and eating relate to getting close to God? God reveals it through his words in The Holy Bible. Come to his table clean and ready to receive.

> **GET READY**

> *'If you're thirsty, come. If you have no money, come. You'll get food and wine and milk without money.' 'Come let me feed you with the heritage of Jacob.' 'Come, I am the living bread... if any man eats this bread, he shall never thirst, never hunger, and will live forever....'* **From** *Isaiah 55, Isaiah 58, John 6 NLT*

It does sound like we're preparing for a meal! Now, let's go back to the beginning of God's story to discover what's on the menu.

"In the beginning was the word and the word was *with God* and the word *was God....* And the word *became flesh* and walked among men." John 1:1,14. AKJV

There's a huge clue here. The word, God's word – The Holy Bible – was with God in the beginning before the creation of this earth. The word was *with* God and the word *was* God. And the word became flesh and walked among men. When it says the word became flesh and walked among men, it refers to Jesus. Jesus is the word of God. Therefore, God is telling us that Jesus is The Holy Bible, God's word, in the flesh. Read it again.

Now, instead of reading very quickly, please just hover here for a minute. Ask yourself, "If Jesus is really the flesh version of The Holy Bible, then how can I know him if I don't know The Holy Bible?"

How can you have a personal relationship with Jesus if you don't know God's word, when in fact, *he* is God's word? When God says, 'draw near to me' he's really saying, 'stop what you're doing, focus on me; find a quiet place and let's talk. If you have questions, I have answers. Read my word.'

Ask God to make himself known to you. Read his word. Talk to him (pray). But understand if you're truly interested in this relationship, you need to be _his_ friend. Are you ready for that kind of commitment? Wash your hands, pull up a chair and come to his table. Feed on the word of God. Prepare your heart for healing and edification.

Reading God's word is a command for God's people, not a suggestion. Many translations of the Bible make it easier to understand; however, sometimes the original meaning is overlooked or left out in the translation. When in doubt, refer to the original Bible - Hebrew for the Old Testament and Greek for the New Testament, or go online and read the scripture in several different versions until you "get" what God is giving. The final test *is* in the Bible – and you need to know what it says. If you disagree with the Bible, tell God and ask him to show you the truth or help you understand.

> *"The seeds that fell along the road are the people who hear the message about the kingdom, but don't understand it. Then the evil one comes and snatches the message from their hearts."*
> **From** *Matthew 13:19 NLT*

HARD TO UNDERSTAND

If it had not been for two great men of God, I would most likely *still* be stumbling around in the Old Testament. It isn't easy to understand at first, but neither is military strategy. The military takes young men out of their comfort zone and puts them through rigorous training and study in order to develop them into a tough team. The *team* is what God's after, but he must develop us one at a time. Our hearts and minds must be focused on God and his goal for the team. *(And I've yet to find any scripture indicating it will be easy.)*

Just a personal comment here - there's something quite mystifying about reading the Bible – at least for me. If I don't read it frequently, I forget it. I memorize a chapter and two months later can't even remember which book it was in. All that work and it's gone! It's not enough to just memorize it, but I have to keep repeating it over and over as often as possible – while driving, mowing, gardening, sewing - whatever! In fact, it's a lot like dieting. There's not a diet out there that will transform you in one session. You have to establish a new pattern of eating only the foods your body needs, and develop the discipline to maintain it. And so it is with reading the Bible. You have to establish a new pattern of taking in God's word on a daily basis to give your spirit the food it needs.

> *To learn, you must love discipline;*
> *it is stupid to hate correction.*
> *Proverbs 12:1 NLT*

DISCIPLINE

This critical part of training is religious repetition. Memorize on a regular basis. Study on a regular basis. Pray on a regular basis. When you do *anything* religiously, it simply means you can be depended upon to do the same thing over and over, time and again. Maybe it's a route you take to work, or maybe it's the time you leave each day. It becomes a habit and habits can be good or bad. Brushing your teeth and washing your face twice a day are good habits. Reading your Bible every day is a very good habit – *even if it's only one verse*. Watching TV just because it's on, or eating just because it's there, are bad habits.

Whenever you create a habit, you create a way of doing things religiously or repeatedly, sometimes without thinking. In building our relationship with God through prayer, we need to break away from the *"without thinking"* portion and create specific focused habits and thoughts that support a healthy life physically, mentally, emotionally and above all, spiritually.

"This book of the law shall not leave your mouth, but you should meditate on it both day and night that you will observe to do according to everything that's written within it, and then you will make your way prosperous and then you will have good success."
Joshua 1:8 WEB

Command from God!

We *are* expected to repeatedly read God's word to improve our relationship with YHVH, as commanded in Joshua 1:8 WEB and Psalm 1. It is our training manual.

However, in Matthew 6:7, Jesus told us *not* to religiously repeat the same prayers over and over again when we pray. Why? Because he doesn't want us to just memorize certain prayers and repeat them in his presence, then get on with our life. He wants us to seek him with our hearts and talk to him personally and then listen for his response.

Be religious, but don't be religious. Repeat, but don't repeat. Feels like a proverb, doesn't it?

Again, God is teaching us how to pray. Follow the *example* Jesus gave in Matthew 6:9-13, but don't *repeat* the same prayer. Talk to him and then listen.

We would not have many friends if we said the same things to them over and over again every time we were with them and then walked off before they could respond. Or what if we went to the doctor's office, explained everything that hurt, asked all kinds of questions, and then left before they could respond to us with therapy or medicine? Wouldn't that be silly?

There are a lot of things God wants us to know so we can better serve him and live an abundant life, *including prayer*, but the number one thing he wants from you is an intimate relationship. To be accepted by him we need to come, clean up, ask forgiveness for our sins, and be his friend. As you make room for him in your heart, he'll do all the work to make you the person he needs you to be.

"You are my friends if you do whatever I command you." *John 15:14 NASB*	**BE A FRIEND**

Being a friend of God, knowing him personally, is YHVH's desire. It's a special privilege. God gives you the freedom to choose; but there are consequences to your choice! God is pursuing your heart, but he's not the only one in pursuit. God is a gentleman and will wait for you to come to him.

However, Satan is pursuing your heart to destroy it, not to heal it. There are only two options; only two suitors. If you do not choose God, Satan *will* rule by default. Without a relationship with YHVH, you have no protection from the wicked one.

YOUR PROTECTION	*"He will protect his godly ones, but the wicked will perish in darkness. No one will succeed by strength alone."* *1 Samuel 2:9 NLT*

Let's face it. We all want a best friend -- a close confidant to share, or connect, with our soul. We want to confide our deepest thoughts and dreams to someone special, knowing they will never make fun of us, or repeat what we've said to someone else. We want someone to share our good times and bad times, joys and troubles, heartaches and, sometimes just to vent!

RELATIONSHIP ATTRIBUTES			

Trusting	Reliable	Accountable	Steadfast
Truthful	Respectful	Confident	Loving
Committed	Honest	Sincere	Listener
Understanding	Passionate	Peaceful	Gracious

God fulfills each of the above attributes and so many more. The question is: '*do those words also describe **our** faithfulness and friendship to God?*' Can he count on us to keep **our** word?

In Ecclesiastes 5:5 he instructs us not to make a promise if we're not going to keep it. Yet there are so many times I've promised him faithfulness, sacrifice, and service and didn't come through. I had good intentions, but got sidetracked or caught up in "stuff" and forgot. Yet he is merciful and forgiving and maintains his faithfulness; continually encouraging us to follow him; to pursue him fervently.

Pursuing God means hunting him down *every* day, reading his word, seeking his will and doing it. Come to him just as you are. Bring all your baggage. Bring your good days and your bad days. Surrender all you have to him. If you truly want to pursue a personal, passionate relationship with God he will change your life. He will take all your pain, all your grief, all your failures and heal you. I don't know how, I just know he does and it doesn't matter where you've been or where you're headed.

ADMIT & SUBMIT

"For all have sinned and come short of the glory of God."

Romans 3:23 KJV

There are several ways God changes us and they all begin with our heart. When you ask God to forgive you and ask Jesus, the Christ, to fill you with his love and give you wisdom and direction, you become a new creation from the inside out.

We all have those things we don't want anyone else to ever know about. We have closets that need to be cleaned out. We have dirty laundry. We need someone to save us from ourselves. And when we clean up and come to God with our heart, he forgives, cleanses, heals and renews our total character.

What can you expect? The closest thing I can think of to help explain the 'before and after' change in a person who has accepted Christ, would be to compare the ghettos of New York City to the mountains of Montana.

In New York City ghettos, gangs control the streets. Masses of people crowd into small, dirty apartments with drugs, poverty and abuse. Children are always crying, teens cursing and adults fighting against a background of sirens and bumper-to-bumper traffic. They didn't choose to be born into poverty and abuse. They each have their own story. They want to be the heroes and heroines but, as Jesus put it, they have a sandy foundation. They need a solid rock for a good foundation and they don't know where to go to find one.

"Whoever listens to me is like a man who built a house and dug deep and laid the foundation on a rock; and when a flood arose, the stream beat vehemently upon that house and could not shake it; for it was founded upon a rock. Luke 6:48 NKJV

A SOLID ROCK

Imagine growing up
in New York City.

and then
moving
to Montana.

Think about it. Imagine growing up in a New York City ghetto. The environment itself would firmly frame a set of standards and expectations for your entire life's core values. Suddenly moving to Montana would change everything! Clean air, singing birds, pure gentle breezes, beautiful sunrises and sunsets, peace and quiet! The whole world you grew up in suddenly disappears. You're standing on a solid rock. It might take awhile to settle in and find direction, but you're a whole new person with all kinds of new opportunities.

"Therefore, if any man is in Christ, he is a new creation; old things are passed away; behold, all things are become new."
2 Corinthians 5:17 NASB1995

ALL NEW

Everything you knew changed, clearly leaving a dramatic passion, energy, purity and power within. You now understand New York City, and can return for a time, but don't be surprised if your heart belongs in Montana.

And so it is with God. Once we've stepped into His presence and met him personally, we can go back to New York City, but Montana will forever be in our hearts. When we totally surrender and ask God to forgive our sins, wipe the slate clean, come into our hearts and make us brand new servants of Christ, he does not dilly-dally around. He's there in a nano-second and it's done.

Surrender!

"But as many as received him, to them he gave power to become the children of God."
John 1:12 AKJV

Growing up on a farm, I spent a lot of time alone. I wasn't lonely, just alone. There's a great difference. Talking to God was quite normal for me, because no one else was around most of the time. As far as outside entertainment goes, our first television was black & white.

It was an ugly olive green square metal box [maybe 12 inches]. We watched Ed Sullivan on Sunday nights. At thirteen I got my first AM transistor radio and on a clear day The Beatles came in fairly well, but most days there was a lot of static since we lived so far from the radio station. That was pretty much it for the entertainment world at our house.

There were, however, a lot of things to do on the farm including walking in the woods, feeding the cows, playing in the hay loft, climbing trees, making mud pies and talking to frogs and worms. Did you know the easiest way to get nightcrawlers *(really big worms for fishing)* is to take a flashlight and bucket down the fence row on a warm summer night and shine the light on the ground? Amazingly huge night crawlers sprawl out on top of the dew-soaked grass just waiting to be plopped into the bucket with some dirt!

Looking back, I wouldn't trade those days for anything. Day by day, in the solitude of those one-on-one hours with God, he drew me into our own very special personal relationship. I had a question – I asked him and he showed me. I had a broken heart – I climbed up on his lap and cried while he held me.

Why am I telling you these things? Because perhaps the most vital step in a personal relationship – being a friend - is to spend *quality* time together. The more time you spend talking to a person, the more you know what's on their heart – what's important to them. Quality time means quiet time where both you and your friend talk and listen to one another.

How can we understand God if we don't know him personally, and why is it so important? Because to understand our own story *(the things that have happened in our lives so far)* we need to understand His story, or his plan for our lives. *[His Story - Do you suppose that's how they came up with the word "history"?]*

As we digest recorded events over the past 6,000 years, we gain truth, knowledge, and understanding. We begin to see the path he has clearly set before us. Setting aside time with God *alone,* to listen for direction and hear his gentle words, is critical. God is in control and is working through you to complete his good plan for your life.

Years ago a car turned very sharply in front of me and I crashed into it, totaling both cars. I was furious. I sat there and pretty much yelled at God, *"I THOUGHT YOU WERE GOING TO PROTECT ME!!!"* And suddenly there was this quiet little voice that said, *"You're not hurt, are you?"* Ouch! I was fuming! The officer thought I was in shock. But no, while I *was* upset about crashing our new used car, I was *furious* about relinquishing my pride. It was a 1972 Buick Electra with all the options and now it was gone. God knew my pride needed an adjustment. More than that, he was in control and he was protecting me, even though I wasn't happy surrendering to his control over my plan and getting on with his plan. I was stuck in the mud again and reminded that my life needed to be totally in God's hands.

Never once has there been a time that I've cried out to God and he's said, *"Oh, I'm so sorry, I didn't know that was going to happen!"*

If things don't go the way you want them to, it doesn't mean God isn't loving, watching or teaching you.

There's more. When you need a best friend, he's there. In fact sometimes he goes over the top.

On Friday, April 9, 2004, I drove to work as usual and parked my Blazer (*the Blaze*) in the parking garage. At the end of the day, I realized I didn't have my car keys and was sure I'd left them in the Blaze. Nope – at least not hanging in the ignition. I checked all pockets, emptied my purse *(cleaned it out while I was at it – doesn't happen often)*, walked back to the office and searched every nook and cranny – nothing.

My husband, bless his heart, drove 25 miles one way back to town and brought the spare key. Ugh. I tried to remember every move I made and came up with total blanks. When I got home I did a quick search in the Blaze but didn't find them.

The next morning I conducted a *thorough* search in the Blaze and, still finding nothing, looked into options for getting a replacement key (geesh they're expensive!) I kept retracing each step in my mind and was getting increasingly upset for not paying more attention and being more responsible.

Driving to church Sunday morning, *using the spare key*, I had a little chat with God. I was still venting and upset with myself and apologized for bothering him with this little item. It was a bit frustrating because I knew that *he* knew exactly where they were.

So I said, *"Now, Lord, I know that you know where my keys are, because you know everything, so would you please just tell me where they are and I'll go get them. Ok? Please?"*

He didn't say a word, but he was there. I arrived at service early and just stopped worrying about the keys. I got out of the Blaze, locked it, took the key, and went on to service. God knew where those keys were and if he wanted me to get them back, he'd tell me where they were.

After service I went back to the Blaze and clicked the spare key fob button to unlock the driver's door. I opened the door, and guess what was lying in the middle of the driver's seat? The keys I lost Friday!

The Blaze was quite spotless after the thorough cleaning the day before but there they were, smack dab in the middle of the black leather driver's seat.

Undoubtedly that was the most humbling experience of my life. In awe and unbelief, I stood there crying and shaking, telling God he didn't have to bring them to me – I could have gone and gotten them – but *"thank you!"*

The only person who knew I'd lost my keys was my husband, and I had the only spare key. When I got home, I asked Phil if, by chance, he'd found the keys and had taken them to the Blaze, opened the door and laid them on the seat and then locked it again and come back home. He looked at me as if I'd finally lost my mind and said, *"What are you talking about? I haven't seen your keys!"* When I told him what happened, he just smiled and shook his head. And I cried.

This was not about lost keys. This was about relationship. Many of you will think it was ridiculous to even have had this conversation with God. Some of you will think I was wasting God's time because he's so busy with other, more important things. Some of you will think I'm delusional. I think God was happy to respond to my request, even though I was only half serious about it to begin with. Why?

As a parent, have you ever done something wonderful for your child that they didn't expect, but you wanted to just because you loved them? As a friend, have you ever gone out of your way to do something your best friend really appreciated? How did it make *you* feel?

As you build your relationship with God, he will touch your heart and you will touch his. He has great plans for you – and they're better plans than you have for you!

GOD KNOWS	*"For I know the plans I have for you," declares YHVH, "plans to prosper you and not to harm you, plans to give you hope and a future."* Jeremiah 29:11 NIV

To understand the plans God has for you, learn how to walk with him. Enter into a very personal relationship with God and stay connected to his power through his word. Discover his heart, his concerns, his expectations, and the image in which you were created.

Understanding his heart will open your eyes to things unseen and pull faith right down under your feet like a solid rock.

Understanding his passion will bring wisdom and grace.

Understanding his expectations will bring you to your knees when you realize all he has done for you, simply hoping you will want to walk with him and be his friend.

Understanding his image will empower you to be all you were created to be.

Discovering your role in His story is critical to developing a powerful, personal relationship with him through prayer. The goal is to have such a close personal relationship with him that no matter the circumstance, no matter what happens in your life, you'll feel the strong foundation beneath your feet, and *know* God is in control at all times, in all circumstances.

"… I remember the devotion of your youth, how as a bride you loved me and followed me through the desert, through a land not sown." Jeremiah 2:2b NIV

God's Cherished Bride
Love and Follow

Jeremiah was God's prophet sent to remind Israel of God's passion for her; for their need to repent, turn from their wicked sins, and fall in love with God all over again; pursue him as a passionate lover as they once did.

Israel rejected God's love *and* his prophets. So God came, in the person of Jesus, to show us his love, to teach us his word, to lay down his life and pay the penalty we deserved, so that not only Israel could come to him, but anyone, everyone.

He is calling us to fall in love with him in a precious and intimate relationship. He is calling us to be his passionate bride.

Begin with a more powerful prayer life – *many conversations with God* - all day long, any and all subjects. Read his word. Learn his story; understand the image you were created in and the power God has given you through his word.

JUST DO IT!

"This book of the law shall not depart out of your mouth, but you shall meditate therein both day and night that you will observe to do according to all that is written therein; for then <u>you</u> shall make your way prosperous and then you shall have good success."

Joshua 1:8 NKJV

"Blessed is the man that walks not in the counsel of the ungodly, nor stands in the way of sinners,

nor sits in the seat of the scornful.

But his delight is in the law of the LORD;

and in his law does he meditate day and night.

And he shall be like a tree planted by the rivers of water, that brings forth his fruit in his season;

his leaf also shall not wither; and whatever he does shall prosper."

Psalm 1:1-3 NKJV

Thoughts:

- Why does God compare his relationship to Israel (*and us*) as that of a newlywed bride and groom?

- If God described his relationship with you, what words would he use?

- According to John 1:1,14 and Revelation 19:13, Jesus is the word of God. In John 14:6 he says, "No one can come to the Father except through me." What does this mean to you?

- Should God answer prayers that are contrary to his word? How will you know if your prayers are contrary to his word?

- What habits help build your relationship with God?

"For your Creator will be your husband; the Lord of Heaven's Armies is his name! He is your Redeemer, the Holy One of Israel, the God of all the earth." Isaiah 54:5 NLT

The Battle

"Do not be afraid nor dismayed …… for the battle is not yours, but God's.
II Chronicles 20:15b KJV

A huge spiritual battle is taking place right now and you have a warrior's role to learn and fulfill. To prepare, you must understand three strategies – yours, your enemy's, and most importantly, God's. God has already given you power to achieve ultimate victory!

Every morning God's artwork compels "ooohhhs" and "aaahhhs" as the sun rises in the early hours with vibrant yellow streaks beaming out from behind narrow slices of orange and violet clouds. The heavens are shouting, *"GLORY TO GOD!"* Each fragrant flower and majestic snowcapped mountain sings of his love and devotion to us.

Then silently and suddenly, through the whispering shadows, evil enters to steal the attention of God's beloved. And so it continues through the ages.

As *I* look back through the ages, subtle evil entered *a lot* – I was always getting in trouble. Satan is sneaky. He doesn't tempt us with big sins in the beginning – just a little distraction – something to make someone upset with us, or gossip about us, or make us feel depressed, defeated or insecure.

Every time I tried to help with a project I messed it up. Like the time I tried to change a wall plug and was ready to stick a metal handled screwdriver onto a bare wire in that little box when my husband let out a war hoop. I don't know what the fuss was all about. I turned off the wall switch! Who was to know that wouldn't work?

And then there was the time I decided to fix the frame of our back door. All it needed was two new 1x4's on each side of the doorjamb. I cut them the right size and then pried out the first one and zipped in the new one. Good job! Then I took off the door and the hinges, but when I tried to pry out the other 1x4 it didn't come out that easily. Go figure. So I started whacking it with the claw side of the hammer until it was fairly destroyed. Then I realized it was the 2x4 supporting the wall! There was no way to put the door back on by this point. Imagine my husband's expression as he arrived moments later and reminded me we had to go to the airport to pick up my parents. He furiously nailed the door to the wall and I later called Sears and paid some big bucks to fix that one!

Even though my heart is in the right place, I have a knack for messing up things, particularly in the area of relationships. This continual battle seems to impact every move I make.

BUT GOD, bless his heart, never leaves me. God is so patient and so good!

In the late 80's we had an old white pickup truck with a broken gas gauge and no money to fix it. We 'gauged' it by some mode of guessing when it should be close to empty. We'd been driving it longer than I thought was safe, but my husband *knew* we had enough. I was getting really nervous about it and ok, so I mentioned it once too often. And then it happened. We were taking our son, Matt, to school and halfway there we ran out of gas. Oh, the words that came out of my husband's mouth weren't anything like those God used to create the world! Matt got out and decided it would be best for him to walk to school, so he took off walking to the east. My husband slammed the door and started walking home, to the west. I just sat in the middle of the seat shaking nervously with tears welling up, asking God what to do.

Just then an old '*woodie*' station wagon pulled off about 50 feet in front of our truck and an elderly man in baggy khaki pants, a red flannel shirt with suspenders and a khaki golf cap got out, opened the back door of the '*woodie*' and brought out a gas can. I couldn't take my eyes off of him. He looked like a plump version of George Burns in the movie, <u>*Oh God.*</u>

This man shuffled when he walked and it seemed to take him forever. As he walked up to the truck I got out, but I couldn't say anything. No words would come. He said, "It looks like you're in trouble, sweetheart!" With tears I nodded 'yes' as he handed me the can of gas. Then he said, "Do you know where Bob Evans is by the interstate?" and I assured him

I did. He said, "Just drop off the can there and I'll pick it up later," and then he shuffled back to his car and drove off leaving me standing there with the gas can.

I started yelling, screaming and waving to my husband, Phil, who finally looked back in disgust, only to see me standing there with a gas can in my hand and no one else around. As he walked back to the truck, still angry, but now confused, he took the can and emptied it into the gas tank and we drove on up the road and picked up Matt while I explained what happened. We took Matt to school and then filled the truck – and the gas can.

There was a lot of silence, then questions. Phil argued over and over that we could *not* drop off a full can of gas at a public restaurant. I didn't know what to say. I didn't know if that was illegal or not, but told him the man was nice enough to bring the gas; the least we could do was refill the can and drop it off as he asked. He was still arguing the restaurant would not take the can when we pulled up to the front door. I took it in, told the lady at the desk a man had asked me to leave it there; she smiled and said, "Thank you."

Several miles and a lot of silence later, Phil asked me what I thought. I said, 'I think God knew I was in trouble and came to help me.'

MY NEED	*"But my God shall supply all your need according to his riches in glory by Christ Jesus." Philippians 4:19 KJV*

Satan knows that if he can destroy our self confidence, he can destroy our relationships. If he can destroy our relationships, he can destroy our families. If he can destroy our families, he can mess with our personal relationship to God and win the battle.

Satan knows we won't fall for things we know are wrong. So, he reminds us of our past, our inadequacies, and drills us on our mistakes – how we'll never amount to anything. Nothing will ever work out for us. We're not special. We're just sinners worthy of all the problems that come our way. Life should be easy. We should relax – we owe it to ourselves. Don't sweat the small stuff – compromise – just a little. Be a team player. Sure, reading the Bible and going to church is very important – just not right now. Besides, you're not feeling that well and you might make someone else sick. You need your rest. You can do it tomorrow – or next week. One thought at a time – if he can convince you, he can destroy you. That's his full time job.

Why does Satan so fervently desire to destroy us?

Lucifer was apparently one of God's most adorned angels. However, he sinned and God reassigned him to be cursed until the final judgment, at which time he will be no more. His pride, dishonesty and violence triggered his transforming plunge from a very beautiful angel into a condemned dragon.

Lucifer

"You were the model of perfection, full of wisdom and exquisite in beauty. You were in Eden, the garden of God. Your clothing was adorned with every precious stone – red carnelian, pale-green peridot, white moonstone, blue-green beryl, onyx, green jasper, blue lapis lazuli, turquoise, and emerald— all beautifully crafted for you and set in the finest gold. They were given to you on the day you were created. I ordained and anointed you as the mighty angelic guardian. You had access to the holy mountain of God and walked among the stones of fire. You were blameless in all you did from the day you were created until the day evil was found in you. Your rich commerce led you to violence, and you sinned. So I banished you in disgrace from the mountain of God. I expelled you, O mighty guardian, from your place among the stones of fire. Your heart was filled with pride because of all your beauty. Your wisdom was corrupted by your love of splendor. So I threw you to the ground and exposed you to the curious gaze of kings. You defiled your sanctuaries with your many sins and your dishonest trade. So I brought fire out from within you, and it consumed you. I reduced you to ashes on the ground in the sight of all who were watching. All who knew you are appalled at your fate. You have come to a terrible end, and you will exist no more."
Ezekiel 28:13b-19 NLT

And the great dragon was cast out, that old serpent, called the Devil, and Satan, which deceived the whole world: he was cast out into the earth, and his angels were cast out with him.

Revelation 12:9 KJV

THE DRAGON

Needless to say, Satan is not a happy camper. His everyday "goal" is to destroy you, or at least a small part of you, to make sure *you* will suffer in the same state, same fate, he's in. If he can't be glorified by God and be with him throughout eternity, he wants to make sure you won't be either.

"Stay alert! Watch out for your great enemy, the devil. He prowls around like a roaring lion, looking for someone to devour. Stand firm against him, and be strong in your faith. Remember that your Christian brothers and sisters all over the world are going through the same kind of suffering you are."

1 Peter 5:8-9 NLT

YOUR ENEMY

YOUR BATTLE

"For we wrestle not against flesh and blood, but against principalities, against powers, against the rulers of the darkness of this world, against spiritual wickedness in high places."

Ephesians 6:12 KJV

This wicked, destructive strategy is deliberately planned to destroy you, one thought at a time. In addition to compromising you right out of God's word, *and your inheritance*, he also has a goal of destroying you physically. To help us understand, God has created many analogies and symbolisms so we can compare the physical with the spiritual.

For instance, look at what your physical heart represents. It is a pump. It pumps blood. Without the heart pumping blood, the body ceases to function – totally.

Blood is composed of red cells, white cells, platelets and plasma. The majority of the content of blood is <u>red cells</u> and one of their main duties is to rush to aid in a crisis. They carry oxygen from the lungs to the body's tissues. You cannot survive without oxygen.

The body's <u>white cells</u> rush to fight off foreign bodies, and/or infection. There are five types of white cells and each of them responds appropriately, according to their purpose, to the fight against the foreign bodies.

<u>Platelets</u>, the smallest of the cellular elements of blood, are critical in the blood clotting process.

<u>Plasma</u> serves as transportation for all these cells: glucose, lipids, amino acids, hormones, metabolic end products, carbon dioxide and oxygen.

Now back to Genesis - Class 101. The blood of the lamb. Abel's sacrifice. God's blood covenant with Abram – all foreshadowing the shed blood of Christ on the cross. The blood of Christ is *extremely* powerful.

- "And so Jesus also suffered outside the city gate to make the people holy **through his own blood.**" Hebrews 13:12 NIV

- "But now in Christ Jesus you who once were far away have been brought near **through the blood of Christ.**" Ephesians 2:13 NIV

- "Therefore, brothers, since we have confidence to enter the Most Holy Place **by the blood of Jesus,** by a new and living way opened for us through the curtain, that is, his body, and since we have a great priest over the house of God, let us draw near to God with a sincere heart in full assurance of faith...." Hebrews 10:19-22 NIV

- "You have come to God, the judge of all men, to the spirits of righteous men made perfect, to Jesus the mediator of a new covenant, and to **the sprinkled blood that speaks a better word than the blood of Abel.** See to it that you do not refuse him who speaks." Hebrews 12:23-25 NASB

- "This then is the message which we have heard of him, and declare unto you, that God is light, and in him is no darkness at all. If we say that we have fellowship with him, and walk in darkness, we lie, and do not the truth: But if we walk in the light, as he is in the light, we have fellowship with one another, and **the blood of Jesus, his Son, purifies us** from all sin." 1 John 1:5-7 NASB

- "May the God of peace, who **through the blood of the eternal covenant** brought back from the dead our LORD Jesus, that great Shepherd of the sheep, equip you with everything good for doing his will, and may he work in us what is pleasing to him, through Jesus Christ, to whom be glory for ever and ever." Hebrews 13:20-21 NASB

From the very first moment you have a true understanding of the price God paid for your sin, and make a commitment to follow Christ and obey his word, you are covered with *his* blood. It brings eternal life no one can take away.

COVERED!	*"My sheep hear my voice, and I know them, and they follow me: And I give unto them eternal life; and they shall never perish, neither shall any man pluck them out of my hand. My Father, which gave them to me, is greater than all; and no man is able to pluck them out of my Father's hand."*

John 10:27-29 NLT

Just as red blood cells bring life-giving oxygen to your body, Christ's blood brings eternal life to your soul. Your soul cannot survive without the blood of Christ.

Just as your white blood cells fight off foreign bodies and infections in your body, Christ's blood fights off foreign bodies infecting your mind and soul. Covered by the blood of Jesus, the word of God, you inherit dunamis power through his blood to fight off Satan and his evil demons. Dunamis power is that awesome, miraculous power of God, so explosive and life changing, the same word was used to build and define the word *dynamite*!

Just as platelets control bleeding in your body so your heart won't be damaged, Christ's blood keeps you whole, protecting you from the destroyer and preventing damage to your soul. Not because we are worthy, but because we are worth it!

Just as plasma is the vehicle used to carry physical nutrients to your body through the blood, so the Holy Spirit is God's choice to carry spiritual nutrients to your body *and* soul through the dunamis power of God's word and the blood of the Lamb.

POWER IN THE BLOOD	*"Therefore, since the children share in flesh and blood, He Himself likewise also partook of the same, that through death He might render powerless him who had the power of death, that is, the devil, and might free those who through fear of death were subject to slavery all their lives."* *Hebrews 2:14-15 NASB*

Again, God is teaching us. There is a direct connection between the life-giving blood in your body and the powerful sacrifice of God's blood covering for your sin. There is a direct connection between your heart, (*the blood pump*) and your soul, which resides in your mind. God continues to give us analogies to understand his word and his love for us.

"But God shows his anger from heaven against all sinful, wicked people who suppress the truth by their wickedness. They know the truth about God because he has made it obvious to them. For ever since the world was created, people have seen the earth and sky. Through everything God made, they can clearly see his invisible qualities—his eternal power and divine nature. So they have no excuse for not knowing God." *Romans 1:18-20 NLT*	*NO EXCUSE*

When you repent and accept Jesus' payment for your sins, the power you inherit as the blood of Christ spills onto your soul, completely covering and saturating it, proclaims and defines your image as it is reflected from God. It not only is your *freedom* from slavery and bondage, but also is your *gift* to reflect that image of God, to react to the greatness of God as he has revealed it to you, and to walk with him intimately every day in love, sacrifice and obedience.

MORE THAN CONQUERORS	*"Yet amid all these things we are **more than conquerors** and gain a surpassing victory through Him Who loved us."*

Romans 8:37 AMP

Satan is powerless against the blood of Christ, so he will do whatever he can to convince you there is nothing to gain by surrendering to Christ. Extremely clever, he will work slowly and deliberately to break down any connection you try to make with Jesus, the Christ.

Satan is *fully* prepared for battle. He has studied us for thousands of years and knows the exact location of our 'heart & soul' buttons. He has a firm strategy and he is patient.

"But when the Father sends the Advocate as my representative—that is, the Holy Spirit—he will teach you everything and will remind you of everything I have told you." *John 14:26 NLT*	**NO WORRIES**

Again, Satan's strategic attack on your heart begins with a very small suggestion – *just a thought* - about something outside of God's will, and then he tries to make it appear as if it's in God's will. It's followed by temptation, then oppression, obsession and finally possession. And let me tell you, Satan is good at his game. Remember - It's all about relationships.

For instance: Let's say you're going to the mall. It's pouring down rain - and crowded - and you're hunting desperately for a parking spot next to the door because you have all those little kids with you. Just as you spot a driver backing out – prime location – another car zips in and takes your space!

What are you thinking? I know – you're asking God to bless them with health, happiness and abundance on their shopping trip. *Right?* Yep! Me, too!

Satan is very clever. He uses our emotions and our senses to form opinions before we get a chance to begin a relationship. Even if you smile, erase all unpleasant thoughts, and find another spot further from the door, you can count on Satan coming back with another devious opportunity from a different angle. This entire battle for your soul is fought in your mind. Satan is fully prepared and very patient.

One of my dearest battles is going to a restaurant. In my mind I'm confirmed. Salad with grilled chicken and with fat free dressing! ….then I see those scrumptious pictures on the menu and smell the steaks (with onions and mushrooms) sizzling on the grill. I'm still firm with my salad until the moment I order. Then suddenly out of nowhere, the most shocking, ungodly words pop out of my mouth, *"I'll have the ribeye with a baked potato, butter and sour cream, an order of mushrooms on the side (grilled in butter of course) and a side salad with fat free dressing."*

Do you see the strategy? One little suggestion, and I go for it almost every time. If Satan can successfully tempt me to load up my blood with fat and cholesterol and then talk me into a nap instead of a walk, he's one step closer to destroying me through my blood. The sooner he's rid of me, the better!

Have you experienced similar battles? Exercise? Diets? Yard work? Ministry? Bible Study? Financial discipline?

<table>
<tr>
<td>

BATTLE

STRATEGY

</td>
<td>

"Joyful are people of integrity, who follow the instructions of the LORD. Joyful are those who obey his laws and search for him with all their hearts. They do not compromise with evil, and they walk only in his paths. You have charged us to keep your commandments carefully. Oh, that my actions would consistently reflect your decrees! Then I will not be ashamed when I compare my life with your commands. As I learn your righteous regulations, I will thank you by living as I should! I will obey your decrees. Please don't give up on me!"

Ps 119:1-8 NLT

</td>
</tr>
</table>

So how does one fight the battle against this evil one?

Turn to Matthew 4. Jesus went to the wilderness where he fasted for 40 days and nights and afterwards was really hungry. Satan began a subtle conversation, just a mere suggestion that if Jesus is hungry, he has the power to satisfy his need. He told him *if* he was the Son of God he could simply turn the stones into bread. Obviously, after creating the heavens and the earth, Jesus *could* turn the stones into bread; in fact on occasion he took a few loaves of bread and a couple fish and fed a multitude of people, so we know he had the power to do it. But he didn't. Why?

Jesus was teaching us how to deal with Satan. Watch what he said in verse 4. **"But it is written…."** And then Jesus quoted Deuteronomy 8:3 NKJV, *"Man shall not live by bread alone, but by every word that proceeds out of the mouth of God."*

Satan didn't give up. He took Jesus to the highest pinnacle of the Temple and told Jesus that *"if"* he was the Son of God, he should jump off… **"because it is written…"** and then Satan quoted Psalm 91:11-12 NKJV, *'…he will give his angels charge over you, to keep you in all your ways. They will catch you in their hands if you even trip over a stone.'*

I told you he was good at his game! Jesus quoted God's word to Satan, so Satan tried to tempt Jesus – quoting God's word!

Jesus didn't argue with him, but simply said, *"**It is written** again, thou shalt not put the* L<small>ORD</small> *your God to the test."* Matthew 4:7 DLNT.

Then Satan took him to a high mountain and showed him all the land as far as he could see. And Satan told Jesus if he would fall down and worship him, Satan would give him everything he could see.

Jesus could have said a lot of things, but basically said *'Get out of here, Satan!* ***For it is written****... you shall worship YHVH, your God, and him only shall you serve.'*

Not just once, but *three times* Jesus is teaching us how to respond to Satan's suggestions. The message is clear. Do not *discuss* anything with Satan! <u>Your power is in the word of God</u>.

If we are quick enough to know Satan is making a suggestion, we can stand on God's word, even quote it out loud, and avoid the temptation. If you block the suggestion and drop it, then you avoid the temptation, and Satan can't cause you to be oppressed by it, or be obsessed with it, and he cannot possess you through it.

Unfortunately, I'm not that quick. Usually I end up thinking, *'Hhmm... that's a pretty good idea'* until I recognize which path I'm on. Then I end up backtracking and quoting like crazy! It happens.

But *you must know God's word* in order to function in the image in which you're created and to be able to use its power in your battle.

In Deuteronomy 34:5-7, we are told that when Moses was 120 years old, he died, and God buried him in a valley, but nobody knows where. And, by the way, as far as we know God didn't personally bury anyone else!

The Book of Jude, the next to last book of the Bible, was written by Jesus' brother, Jude. Stay with me – there's a connection.

In Jude 9 *(there's only one chapter in the Book of Jude, so there isn't a chapter number)*, Jude is, again, following Jesus' lead giving us yet another clue about our interactions with Satan. Satan was speaking to Michael, God's warrior archangel, and it appears there was a disagreement about the body of Moses. We're told Michael 'did not *dare* accuse Satan.' All he said was, *"The L*ORD *rebuke you!"* Jude 9 NIV

Are we connecting the dots yet?

*"By the **word** of the L*ORD *were all the heavens made…."* Psalm 33:6a AKJV

*"Man shall not live by bread alone, but by every **word** that proceeds out of the mouth of God."* Deuteronomy 8:3 NKJV

*"Through faith we understand that the worlds were framed by the **word** of God, so that things which are seen were not made of things which appear."* Hebrews 11:3 AKJV

*"For **he spoke**, and it was done; **he commanded**, and it stood fast."* Psalm 33:9 NASB

*"So shall my **word** be that goes forth out of my mouth; it shall not return to me void, but it shall accomplish that which I please and it shall prosper in the thing I sent it to do."* Isaiah 55:11 NKJV

"Let us create man in our image." Genesis 1:26a NKJV

In Romans 4:17 <u>we</u> are instructed to 'Call those things that <u>are not</u>, as though they were' so that they will be. The command is to speak the things not yet confirmed in our lives, so they <u>will be</u> confirmed in our lives, i.e., healing, salvation, peace, grace, etc., by the word of God.

Both Michael *and* Jesus are full of power and yet even so, when confronted by Satan, they *only* respond by quoting God's powerful word. We should, therefore, follow their example and take the advice of James, another of Jesus' brothers, *"Submit yourselves to God. Resist the devil and he will flee from you."* James 4:7 AKJV.

The next time someone cuts you off in traffic or takes your prime space, ask God to protect them from the evil one and to bless them and draw them ever closer to God through his Spirit and his word. Not only will you win the battle, but you'll leave a powerful legacy for those little ears in the back seat.

PRAY FOR OTHERS	*"My prayer is not that you take them out of the world but that you protect them from the evil one."* *John 17:15 NIV*

But is quoting God's word all that's required?

Please turn to Ephesians 6. Here we're instructed to put on the whole armor of God so that we can stand up against Satan's battle tactics. We're not at war with physical things; it's a war against principalities, powers, this world's rulers of darkness, and spiritual wickedness in high places.

Ephesians 6:14-18 KJV	Specific instructions:
Stand, having your loins girded about with truth, and	1. Wrap yourself up in the truth
Having on the breastplate of righteousness, and	2. Wash your hands and clean up your heart
Your feet shod with the preparation of the gospel of peace;	3. Find the peace of God and walk in it
Above all, taking the shield of faith with which you can quench all the fiery darts of the wicked, and	4. Have faith in God – trust him for all things so that nothing will penetrate or damage your faith, but rather will ensure victory
Take the helmet of salvation,	5. Surrender to Jesus and embrace salvation
Take the sword of the Spirit, *which is the word of God*, **praying always** with all prayer and supplication in the Spirit.	6. Speak the word of God, praying always

Look at Paul's picture of this warrior. Paul is instructing us to be strong in the LORD and in the power of his might by putting on this armor. Notice our only action appears to be *preparation*. No physical fighting, just get prepared and **STAND**.

"STAND, HAVING YOUR LOINS GIRDED ABOUT WITH TRUTH....."

EPHESIANS 6:14a KJV

"Do not be afraid nor dismayed ..... for the battle is not yours, but God's.

You shall not need to fight in this battle: set yourselves,

stand still, and see the salvation of the LORD"

II Chronicles 20:15, 17 KJV

> **JUST STAND**

Take a closer look at this Ephesians 6 warrior. The term "loins" was a reference to a very powerful part of the body from the waist to the thighs. To gird the loins with garments indicated a readiness to travel, or to make special preparation for the journey. Paul begins by telling us to stand, with our loins girded about [*wrapped up*] in the truth. How do you wrap yourself up in the **truth**?

In John 14:6 KJV, Jesus said, *"I am the way, <u>the truth</u> and the life, no man comes to the Father but by me."* Jesus said *he* is the truth; you *must* find him if you want to be embraced by, and have communion with God!

Jesus is *the word* according to John 1:1,14 KJV: *"In the beginning was the Word, and the Word was with God, and <u>the Word was God</u>... and the Word was made flesh, and dwelt among us".*

In Revelation 19:13 KJV John said, referring to Jesus, *"and his name is called The Word of God."*

So, therefore, if Jesus is the word of God, and Jesus is the truth, then we should see that the truth *is* the word of God. And now you know exactly what to wrap yourself up in!

<table>
<tr><td>

FIND

THE

TRUTH!

</td><td>

"Their minds are full of darkness; they wander far from the life God gives because they have closed their minds and hardened their hearts against him. They have no sense of shame. They live for lustful pleasure and eagerly practice every kind of impurity. But that isn't what you learned about Christ.

You have heard him, and have been taught by him; <u>the truth is in Jesus</u>. Throw off your old sinful nature and your former way of life, which is corrupted by lust and deception. Instead, let the Spirit renew your thoughts and attitudes". Ephesians 4:18-23 NLT

</td></tr>
</table>

"....HAVING ON THE BREASTPLATE OF RIGHTEOUSNESS"
EPHESIANS 6:14b KJV

Next is the **breastplate of righteousness**. The breastplate protects the heart. The heart is the main target of the battle. So how do you become **righteous**?

Abraham was God's friend. In 2 Chronicles 20:7, we're told God gave the Promised Land to the seed of Abraham, who was *God's friend*. Again in Isaiah 41:8 we find God calls Israel his servant, the seed of Abraham, [who is] *"my friend"*. And in James 2:23 NASB, *"And the scripture was fulfilled which said, Abraham believed God, and it was counted unto him for righteousness; and he was called* the *friend of God."*

<table>
<tr><td>

RIGHTEOUSNESS

</td><td>

If we confess our sins, he is faithful and just to forgive us our sins and to cleanse us from all unrighteousness.

1 John 1:9 KJV

</td></tr>
</table>

Believe God and be his friend!

"AND YOUR FEET SHOD WITH THE PREPARATION OF THE GOSPEL OF PEACE…"
EPHESIANS 6:15 KJV

Paul's letter to the Colossians, chapter 3, tells us how to have **peace**. If we accept the blood Christ gave for our sins, we should try to think like he thinks and focus on things above, not on the things of this earth. We should put away all anger and maliciousness, stop filthy words from coming out of our mouths, and stop lying. What goes in is what comes out, so fill yourself with the things of God. We should be renewed, walk in the image in which we were created, and be tender, merciful, kind, humble, meek and patient. And above all we should love one another and let the peace of God rule in our hearts.

But why prepare your *feet* with peace? Remember it's all about relationships! Wherever you go, whenever you talk to friends and neighbors or total strangers, God may be using you to draw them closer to him. Walk in the blood of Jesus and leave footprints wherever you go!

PEACE

"And the peace of God, which passes all understanding, shall keep your hearts and minds through Christ Jesus."

Philippians 4:7 KJV

"ABOVE ALL, TAKING THE SHIELD OF FAITH

WITH WHICH YOU CAN QUENCH ALL THE FIERY DARTS OF THE WICKED…."

EPHESIANS 6:16 KJV

The warrior's shield is made of impenetrable metal to knock down fiery arrows and prevent fatal wounds. Your shield of **faith** in God must be strong and confident.

Faith can be a confusing word, a lot like the word, 'believe.' For a long time I thought to have faith, or to believe, in God was to know him, but then I found that scripture saying the demons believe and tremble, and *they* know him. They know who he is and believe he is God, but they are not his friends.

Maybe faith doesn't have the impact it should because we use it to mean so many things. We call religion our faith. We have faith in people, or in ourselves or equipment, which ultimately fails. But when you have as much **faith** in God as you do the chair you're sitting in, that's the faith Paul's talking about. Believing is good. Knowing is good. But having faith in God as your best friend – it doesn't get any better.

BE ALERT – WATHFOR THOSE ARROWS!

"Behold, I send you forth as sheep in the midst of wolves: be ye therefore wise as serpents, and harmless as doves."

Matthew 10:16 KJV

"TAKE THE HELMET OF SALVATION..."

EPHESIANS 6:17A KJV

Salvation is understanding the sin we were born into and accepting the terms of God's payment for our sins, his death on the cross, the precious sacrificed Lamb of God. We were raised into spiritual slavery and God bought us out of it; he redeemed us. To 'redeem' is to 'buy back'. We were once his before we were lost in sin, and now he offers to buy us back. He paid a huge price for us, yet he does not insist we come to him. He calls. And waits for our response.

'Salvation' is connected to 'understanding' through your control center, your soul and mind, where all relationship elements reside.

When our son, Matt, was in the third grade, he asked a very pensive question, *"Mother, where is your soul?"* Now I thought this was one of those great teachable moments, and it was, except that it turned out Matt was the teacher. I told him the soul was in the heart of man.

He said, *"Think about it. Your heart is a pump. It pumps blood. Your soul is in your mind. Every thought, good or evil, begins in your mind."*

It is your control center. It is where you fight your battle.

Therefore, *if* your soul is in your mind, and your mind processes all information and decisions, and your mind is the battle ground, doesn't it make sense to completely cover and protect your soul and your mind, in fact your entire head, with the helmet of Salvation?

OPEN UP!	*"Behold, I stand at the door and knock. If anyone hears my voice and opens the door, I will come in to him and will sup with him and he with me.* Revelation 3:20 KJV*

"Take the sword of the Spirit, <u>which is the word of God</u>,

praying always with all prayer and supplication in the Spirit."

Ephesians 6:17b-18a KJV

God's final instruction, after we're prepared for the battle, is to take the sword of the Spirit, which is the **word** of God, and **pray!**

I find it interesting that the sword of the Spirit, or the word of God, is mentioned as the last 'critical gear' part of this warrior. We are to gear up for this huge battle, train and prepare physically, mentally, emotionally and spiritually, and then *what?* **PRAY!** And pray with what? The word of God.

In Revelation 19:15a KJV we're told, *"out of his mouth goes a sharp sword, that with it he should smite the nations…"* The very last battle on earth will be won at the second coming of Jesus, the Christ, solely by speaking with the "sharp sword of the spirit," the word of God. No physical fighting. Powerful final and total victory through merely speaking the word of God!

<table>
<tr><td>

PRAY!

</td><td>

"If my people, which are called by my name, shall humble themselves, and pray, and seek my face, and turn from their wicked ways; then will I hear from heaven, and will forgive their sin, and will heal their land."

2 Chronicles 7:14 KJV

</td></tr>
</table>

Understand yourself, your enemy, your role in the battle, your relationship to God, and then

PRAY!

<u>*Thoughts*</u>:

The Israelites were up against a wall, so to speak, in battle against the Philistines. Saul's son, Jonathan, slipped away from the troops with his armor bearer to check out the situation and the position of the Philistines. *"Let's go across to the outpost of those pagans,"* Jonathan said to *his armor bearer. "Perhaps the LORD will help us, for nothing can hinder the LORD. He can win a battle whether he has many warriors or only a few!"* 1 Samuel 14:6 NLT. As you read the full story in 1 Samuel, you will see God acted in response to Jonathan's words and saved Israel that day.

- Take a few moments to review past battles in *your* life. How did your words impact the outcome of the battle? What about the battles that lay ahead? How can you change the outcome? What words will you use? What will be your dunamis source of power to defeat the enemy?

- God needs you! There will come a day when you will walk with him in eternity. But right now, he needs you, his warrior, to prepare for the battle and defend your family, your neighbors, your friends, your community and your country against the enemy.

FOR THE WORD OF GOD IS ALIVE AND POWERFUL.

IT IS SHARPER THAN THE SHARPEST TWO-EDGED SWORD, CUTTING BETWEEN SOUL AND SPIRIT, BETWEEN JOINT AND MARROW.

IT EXPOSES OUR INNERMOST THOUGHTS AND DESIRES.

HEBREWS 4:12 NLT

Prayer

"I cried to the LORD with my voice and he heard me from his holy hill."

Psalm 3:4 KJV

Prayer is your lifeline to God. Prayer is your power source. The effectiveness of your prayer is the measurement of how deeply you touch the heart of God and create change in your life on a daily basis. Prayer is the gate key to paradise. It is the course and image. It is your passport to salvation. It is your weapon.

The ocean is beautiful. It's a lot of water. But that's probably not the definition an oceanographer would give. It's all in perspective. Because the ocean's surface is much different from the structure beneath, what we see from land doesn't give us the entire picture. When we study the total structure, and begin to look below the surface, we discover an awesome, totally different world. Things are not always what they seem. Is the ocean beautiful? Absolutely! Is it a lot of water? Absolutely! Is there more to learn? Absolutely! And so it is with prayer.

This is the *prayer relationship* that the God of Abraham, Isaac and Jacob wants you to pursue with him. God wants you to dig deep beneath the surface for a more powerful relationship and he will show you mighty and awesome things as you build more effective prayers and better understand the power God has created in you.

Are you ready to fulfill that image? Are you ready to reflect his glory? So how do you start? What do you say?

When I accepted Christ publicly, my biggest fear was that someone would ask me to pray out loud. I didn't know how and didn't want anyone to make fun of me. I'd been talking to God as if he were my best friend, which he was, but I told him I needed to learn how to pray and say all those words I'd heard ministers say.

TEACH ME	*"God has not given us the spirit of fear; but of power, and of love, and of a sound mind."*

2 Timothy 1:7 KJV

But wouldn't it be a whole lot simpler if I could just talk to him in front of other people like I normally did when I was alone? And so it became my prayer.

"Meditate within your heart on your bed and be still."	**MEDITATE**

Psalm 4:4b NASB

The challenge came when people *did* ask me to pray. I was lost. Everything came out wrong and sounded selfish, basically because my whole world revolved around my most current crisis (*and there were many*), so I retreated to the mud once again.

Eventually, sound public praying became inevitable. It was very difficult for me to understand what God wanted me to say because, quite frankly, I didn't get involved with other people. How was I supposed to know what they wanted or needed?

I knew I needed to learn more about God's story and my role in it, so I began to pay close attention to others' prayers. *Sometimes*, though, as I listened to their prayers, I wondered if they knew God was really listening. They started out talking *to* him and then started talking *about* him and then rather left him totally out of the conversation.

Passion for prayer grows with your relationship to God. You *will* find a balance. As you draw closer in relationship to him and expose your true heart, he will heal you and provide for every need in your life. Remember – God is always listening. There is not a right or wrong way to pray. There are not right words and wrong words. He wants to hear from your heart. But he does provide standards for *more effective* prayers.

> *"The effective, fervent prayer of a righteous man availeth much! Elijah was a man subject to like passions as we are, and he prayed earnestly that it might not rain: and it rained not on the earth by the space of three years and six months. And he prayed again, and the heaven gave rain, and the earth brought forth her fruit."*
>
> *James 5:16b-18 KJV*

EFFECTIVE PRAYER

God's word provides a lot of meat for your journey. As you study the Old Testament you'll find men and women of courage who depended upon the power of talking and listening to God and obeying him even when it hurt, like David and Esther and Hezekiah.

A MAN AFTER MY OWN HEART

> *"And when he had deposed him, he raised up David to be their king; of him he bore witness and said, 'I have found David, son of Jesse, a man after my own heart, who will do all my will and carry out my program fully.'"*
>
> *Acts 13:22 AMPC*

David was a shepherd. He spent time alone on the hills with his sheep. He protected his sheep from lions and bears and many other dangers. He had a relationship with his sheep. He talked to them and they knew his voice. He loved them and they loved him. He reflected God's image.

David knew YHVH intimately. All day long he gathered thoughts focused on God. He wrote many Psalms, praising God, seeking God, crying out to God, embracing the foundation that would carry him through all the difficult years of Saul's aggressive pursuit to kill him.

Since God called David, *"A man after my own heart,"* let's check out one of his prayers - Psalm 51 KJV. This prayer was offered to God after Nathan exposed David in his sin with Bathsheba *(Spicy story found in II Samuel 11).*

"Have mercy on me, O God, because of your unfailing love. Because of your great compassion, blot out the stain of my sins. Wash me clean from my guilt. Purify me from my sin. For I recognize my rebellion; it haunts me day and night. Against you, and you alone, have I sinned; I have done what is evil in your sight. You will be proved right in what you say, and your judgment against me is just. For I was born a sinner—yes, from the moment my mother conceived me. But you desire honesty from the womb, teaching me wisdom even there.

Purify me from my sins, and I will be clean; wash me, and I will be whiter than snow. Oh, give me back my joy again; you have broken me—now let me rejoice. Don't keep looking at my sins. Remove the stain of my guilt. Create in me a clean heart, O God. Renew a loyal spirit within me. Do not banish me from your presence, and don't take your Holy Spirit from me.

Restore to me the joy of your salvation, and make me willing to obey you. Then I will teach your ways to rebels, and they will return to you. Forgive me for shedding blood, O God who saves; then I will joyfully sing of your forgiveness. Unseal my lips, O LORD, that my mouth may praise you.

You do not desire a sacrifice, or I would offer one. You do not want a burnt offering. The sacrifice you desire is a broken spirit. You will not reject a broken and repentant heart, O God. Look with favor on Zion and help her; rebuild the walls of Jerusalem. Then you will be pleased with sacrifices offered in the right spirit—with burnt offerings and whole burnt offerings. Then bulls will again be sacrificed on your altar."

David was a sinner – just like you and me. He was overcome with passion for a beautiful woman and when she was found pregnant, he had her husband killed. Should I also mention her husband was one of David's most loyal battle commanders? And yet God called David, *"A man after my own heart."*

David walked with God. Then he fell. *Hard!* Then he got back up in his brokenness and restored his relationship with God. We *all* should reflect this image.

Again, God is teaching us. To offer sacrifice was the law. Cain knew it. David knew it.

What difference between Cain and David prompted banishment for one and eternal life for the other? The condition of their hearts, their obedience, and the power of their words, all of which were contingent upon their relationship to God!

"And Samuel said, 'Hath the LORD as great delight in burnt offer-ings and sacrifices, as in obeying the voice of the LORD? Behold, to obey is better than sacrifice, and to hearken than the fat of rams.'"
1 Samuel 15:22 KJV

LAW **VS** **HEART**

Solomon was the second son of David and Bathsheba. *(The first child died as a direct result of David's sin - blood for blood, remember?)* When Solomon became king, God granted him one wish and he chose wisdom.

WISDOM	*"And God said to Solomon, Because this was in your heart, and you have not asked for riches, wealth, or honor, nor the life of your enemies, neither yet have you asked for long life; but have asked for wisdom and knowledge for yourself, that you may judge my people over whom I have made you king; wisdom and knowledge is granted to you; and I will give you riches, and wealth, and honor, such as none of the kings have had that have been before you, neither shall there any after you have the like."*

II Chronicles 1:11-12 NKJV

As David discovered, failure is a critical element in our lives and often surfaces due to a lack of wisdom. How we *deal* with it impacts our relationship with God. Embrace it; take notes, learn from it, but don't wallow in it. Go to God's word. Find your example and learn from God. *He really is an awesome teacher!*

As you come across scripture that pinpoints your situation, make it your prayer! Take David's prayer as your own. Take Hezekiah's prayer(s) as your own (II Kings 19:15-19 & Isaiah 38:1-5). Mold them around your situation. Build a powerful prayer. Write it down. Memorize it until you connect with the heart of God. Offer it up to God with a sincere and repentant heart.

ELEMENTS OF PRAYER

- Offer true repentance

- Praise him for all his greatness

- Remind him of his promises; quote scripture *(by the way, this is for your benefit – he hasn't forgotten)*

- Ask for cleansing, healing

- Ask him to recreate your heart with willingness and loyal obedience

- Praise him for the awesome teacher he is, that you might reflect his image and walk with him in joy and truth

- Pray for your ministry – those he would have you reach out and touch

- Pray for peace in Jerusalem (Psalm 122:6a NLT)

Why should you look to God's word to build prayers? Because it *is* the word of God! Where is your power? It *is* the word of God! What is your sword for the battle? It *is* the word of God! Read it again. ☺

YOUR **WORDS** & **YOUR HEART**

"My child, pay attention to what I say. Listen carefully to my words. Don't lose sight of them. Let them penetrate deep into your heart, for they bring life to those who find them, and healing to their whole body. Guard your heart above all else, for it determines the course of your life."

Proverbs 4:20-23 NLT

Reflect the image of God by calling those things that are not, as though they were, so that they will be. Isn't that your prayer? Why would you pray for something you already have? Isn't it what you *don't* have that you want?

Did God call Abram *"Abraham"* just for the fun of 2 more letters? No! He called him *"Abraham"* which means 'father of many nations' when it was time for him to *become* the father of many nations. *Reflect his image!* When it's time for your need to be met, call it! God will answer.

Again in Matthew 6:9, Jesus gives us a pattern, or 'manner' of prayer. It was not, however, to be repeated over and over as our own personal "standard prayer." It is an excellent recital for corporate prayer on occasion, but it is not what God wants to hear from you over and over again each morning.

How do I know this? Because two verses before, in Matthew 6:7, Jesus strictly instructs us not to *'repeat'* prayers, because they become vain and meaningless.

There are, of course, exceptions. When you are breaking out of your old habits and building new ones in prayer, you need to do a lot of repeating. *"Meditate on this book of the law both day and night"* as instructed in Joshua 1:8 and Psalm 1:2. You will find a comfort zone in working on your prayers as you study God's word. Again, repeat, but don't repeat.

Do you ever wake up and say, *"Good morning, Father! How was your night? How did your people bless you while I slept and what broke your heart?"* And then, in silence, try to visualize what God saw during the night all over the earth. In America. In Afghanistan. In Egypt. In Australia. In China. In Europe. In Iraq. What blessed him? What broke his heart?

This may not be what comes to mind when you think of prayer, but it should be as we work to build a solid relationship that cares about God and others and not just our own needs.

In contrast, do we wake up each and every day and say, *"Thank you, Father, for today. Bless my family and friends and be with us and watch over us all day. Amen!"*?

When we memorize a phrase and offer it to God, instead of developing a relationship with him, prayers become wish lists: things we want our God to do for us. There may be a few thank you's and a bit of praise, but how often do we think about God's concerns, listen to what he has to say, or try to figure out how we fit into his plan, his story?

The biggest problem with repeating a routine prayer is we miss out on an opportunity to develop our walk with God; build our relationship with him. When we memorize a prayer and say it over and over again, it may lose meaning over time for both the giver and the receiver.

At the same time, the biggest blessing repeating a routine prayer may be in developing a daily habit of coming before the LORD. As parents instruct their children to take time to pray each day, regardless of whether the prayer is memorized or from the heart, they are building solid habits the child will carry throughout his life. Memorizing prayers is an excellent way to begin a powerful prayer life if you've not been in the habit of praying on a daily basis.

As we look at the specific prayer pattern in Matthew, Jesus brings several elements to our attention.

"Pray, then, in this way:

Our Father who is in heaven	• Address ALL prayers to God the Father, whose name is YHVH
Hallowed be Your name	• **Praise** His name
Your kingdom come. Your will be done, on earth as it is in heaven.	• Pray for what God wants
Give us this day our daily bread.	• Pray for what you want
And forgive us our debts, as we also have forgiven our debtors.	• Ask God for Forgiveness
And do not lead us into temptation, but deliver us from evil.	• Ask God for Protection
For Yours is the kingdom and the power and the glory forever."	• **Praise** His name
Amen *Matthew 6:9-13 NKJV*	

Does Jesus' pattern line up with David's? Absolutely! Notice praise is listed twice. First *and* last. Hhmm. Do you think that was a mistake? Or could it be God is teaching us again?

PRAISE HIM

"Offer unto God thanksgiving; and pay your vows unto the most High:

And call upon me in the day of trouble: I will deliver you, and you shall glorify me."

Psalm 50:14-15 KJV

God does not have an ego problem. In fact, in Psalm 50:12 KJV, God says, *"If I were hungry, I would not tell you: for the world is mine, and the fullness thereof."*

God knows who he is. In Isaiah 42:8 KJV he says, *"I am YHVH: that is my name; and my glory will I not give to another, neither my praise to carved images."*

So if God doesn't have an ego problem, and he certainly knows who he is, why do we need to praise him?

Praise transforms our heart and soul like nothing else can! Again, God is teaching us.

In order to function effectively in God's kingdom on earth, in order to become vibrant standing stones pointing others to salvation, in order to become powerful prayer warriors, we need to have our vision adjusted. We need to see God for who he really is. We need to take our eyes off our own problems and focus on God's plan for our lives. We need to re-adjust our vision so often we begin to see out of God's eyes and meet the needs of his people.

Praising YHVH, we can't help but feel lost in his awesome splendor. We can't help but feel hope through his power. We can't help but feel the need to pursue him and fulfill our purpose.

"Let all that I am praise the LORD. *O* LORD *my God, how great you are! You are robed with honor and majesty. You are dressed in a robe of light. You stretch out the starry curtain of the heavens; you lay out the rafters of your home in the rain clouds. You make the clouds your chariot; you ride upon the wings of the wind. The winds are your messengers; flames of fire are your servants. You placed the world on its foundation so it would never be moved. You clothed the earth with floods of water, water that covered even the mountains. At your command, the water fled; at the sound of your thunder, it hurried away. Mountains rose and valleys sank to the levels you decreed. Then you set a firm boundary for the seas, so they would never again cover the earth. You make springs pour water into the ravines, so streams gush down from the mountains. You send rain on the mountains from your heavenly home, and you fill the earth with the fruit of your labor. You made the moon to mark the seasons, and the sun knows when to set. May the glory of the* LORD *continue forever! You, O* LORD *take pleasure in all you have made! The earth trembles at your glance; the mountains smoke at your touch. I will sing to the* LORD *as long as I live. I will praise my God to my last breath! Let all that I am praise the* LORD.*"*

Psalm 104:1-10,13,19,31-33,35 NLT

ADJUST YOUR VISION

Outside of man, all of creation is faithful and obedient to God's commands. As you begin to praise him, think about all God accomplished for *you* in the first 6 days of creation, i.e., seeds. *(Where would we be without seeds? Seeds are amazing!)*

Through powerful space station telescopes, we're just now finding unbelievably beautiful planets and magnificent parts of the universe no man previously knew existed. God's creation inspires awe and wonder. The heavens are shouting, ***"GLORY TO GOD!"*** And so should we!

"I have swept away your sins like a cloud.

I have scattered your offenses like the morning mist.

Oh, return to me, for I have paid the price to set you free.

Sing, O heavens, for the LORD has done this wondrous thing.

Shout for joy, O depths of the earth! Break into song,

O mountains and forests and every tree!"

Isaiah 44:22-23a NLT

SHOUT FOR JOY!

When you're stuck in the mud or buried beneath burdens so deep you don't know how to pray, just begin praising God. Tell him of his excellent greatness! Exalt him for the life you've been given – the oxygen flowing through your blood! Praise him that you don't have to remind your lungs when to breath in and out, or tell your heart when to beat. Praise him for his great plan for his peace in your life.

Reconcile whatever issues stand between you and your relationship with God, and ask him to lead you into a closer, deeper walk with him.

HOPE

"For I know the plans I have for you," says the LORD. "They are plans for good and not for disaster, plans to give you a future and a hope."

Jeremiah 29:11 NLT

Think back to every verse in Genesis 1 that began with, *"And God said....!"* Could God have just *thought* about creation and it would have appeared, without speaking a word? And if so, why did he speak the words out loud?

Again, God is teaching us. In his image *we* need to speak his word out loud. I know, I wasn't comfortable with it at first either. But God was faithful to teach me.

Many years ago within one particular week in my life, four (4) people, individually, called and asked me to pray for them because they had a kidney infection. Of course this raised a red flag and I took the task seriously. I talked to God and asked him to heal them quickly, and he did, however, *I* got a kidney infection. And yes, I went to the doctor.

I was still curious about how this all worked, so I asked the doctor if he believed God could heal people. He said, *"Of course, that's why he gave us doctors,"* and proceeded to issue a prescription for the kidney infection. Not exactly the answer I was looking for.

Even more curious *(and broke)*, I went directly home and didn't fill the prescription. No one else was home, so I began talking out loud to God, something to the effect of, "Ok. Look. I prayed for these people and you healed them. Then I ended up with the kidney infection. Now I know you're all about "fair" but this just doesn't seem to fit. Your word says, *'Jesus was wounded for my transgressions, he was bruised for my iniquities, the chastisement for my peace was on him, and by his stripes I'm healed[4].'* Your word also says, *'Call upon me and go and pray to me, and I will listen to you[5].'* Your word also says, *'Ask and it shall be given to you[6].'* Your word also says to, *'Call those things that are not, as if they were'[7]* so that they will be. Your word also says, *'If you ask anything in my name, I will do it[8].'* I didn't ask for this kidney infection and I'm not accepting it. It has no authority in my body and I'm calling it out. Get out, you kidney infection, you have no authority in my body! Do you hear me? Get out! Get out in Jesus' name!"

Say what you will, there was no sign of a kidney infection the next morning *(or since)*.

---

[4] Isaiah 53:5 KJV
[5] Jeremiah 29:12 NLT
[6] Matthew 7:7 KJV
[7] Romans 4:17 NMB
[8] John 14:14 NKJV

"But God hath chosen the foolish things of the world to confound the wise; and God hath chosen the weak things of the world to confound the things which are mighty; and base things of the world, and things which are despised, hath God chosen, yes, and things which are not, to bring to nought things that are, that no flesh should glory in his presence."

1 Corinthians 1:27-29 KJV

FOOLISH THINGS?

When you hurt badly enough and want healing desperately you won't mind sounding a bit foolish either.

COUNT IT ALL JOY!

"When troubles come your way, consider it an opportunity for great joy. For you know that when your faith is tested, your endurance has a chance to grow. So let it grow, for when your endurance is fully developed, you will be perfect and complete, needing nothing.
If you need wisdom, ask our generous God, and he will give it to you. He will not rebuke you for asking. But when you ask him, be sure that your faith is in God alone. Do not waver, for a person with divided loyalty is as unsettled as a wave of the sea that is blown and tossed by the wind. Such people should not expect to receive anything from the LORD. Their loyalty is divided between God and the world, and they are unstable in everything they do."

James 1:2-8 NLT

As you begin to pray, try to organize your thoughts. Plan your prayer. Think about what you really want and whether it's a valid need, or a bit of fluff. If you're still not sure how to word it, read through the Psalms and Proverbs. Trust me, no matter what your need, someone's already dealt with it. When you come to a verse that "fits" your need, hover over it and make it your prayer.

About the fluff. My past experiences have revealed God's incredible heart to me, in that he knew the fluff in *my* heart, and when I focused on God's word, the fluff came without asking.

We lived in a very small house in a quaint little neighborhood that was quickly going downhill and arrived home one night to discover our house had been broken into and several things were missing. One in particular was a little black and white TV my dad had given me. We called the police and they came and went through the house and searched all around the yard.

I was still confused about my role, so my conversation with God the next morning on the way to work went something like, *"Ok, so I know I'm not to hate whoever did this. Obviously you knew about it, so maybe they needed the stuff more than I did. But did they have to take that TV? My dad gave that to me, you know."* And then I broke down in tears, resolving to accept whatever plan God had for me.

That evening when we got home, the neighbors all came over with their lawn chairs and sat around in the yard, which was the normal nightly procedure. Our oldest son was riding his bike – not too well – and almost hit one of the neighbors. I ordered him to put up the bike, which he did, but then he came running around the house out of breath. *"Mom – the TV's sitting in the back yard! They brought it back!"*

We all ran around and sure enough, there it was sitting on the ground in front of the shed. We called the police and they came. This officer was very puzzled and took fingerprints. He had canvassed the entire area around our house that afternoon and the TV wasn't there. In his frustration he finally told me that this just doesn't happen. *"When thieves take things they sell them or fence them, but they never bring them back! This just doesn't happen!"*

I said, *"I know. I know!"* Then he said, *"No! You don't understand."* But I did.

REQUESTS

Be anxious for nothing, but in everything by prayer and supplication with thanksgiving, let your requests be made known to God.

Philippians 4:6 NKJV

Notice the instruction in the verse above: *don't worry* about anything, but *pray* about everything and *"let your requests be made known to God."* Let your <u>requests</u> – not your PROB-LEMS, but your <u>requests</u> - be made known to God.

"Can all your worries add a single moment to your life? And if worry can't accomplish a little thing like that, what's the use of worrying over bigger things? Look at the lilies and how they grow. They don't work or make their clothing, yet Solomon in all his glory was not dressed as beautifully as they are. And if God cares so wonderfully for flowers that are here today and thrown into the fire tomorrow, he will certainly care for you."

Luke 12:25-28 NLT

DON'T WORRY

As you focus on what you want and need from God, remember he's not only your Father, he's your friend. But more than a father and friend, he knows everything about you. He knows your pain and your joy. He knows your need and your dreams. He understands who you are and he knows who you need to be in order to fill your role and take your position in the battle. He knows how to take care of you.

You don't have to fill him in on all that's going on in your life and how miserable and unhappy you are. He knows these things already, and has given you dunamis power to overcome them by calling things that are *not*, via Romans 4:17. Telling him about the yuck you're going through is not only a waste of time, but as you are speaking, you're confirming your yuck.

In addition to scripture, you can build upon prior prayers that have meaning for you, or simply prayers you learned long ago. The first prayer I learned as child went something like this:

Now I lay me down to sleep. I pray the LORD my soul to keep. If I should die before I wake, I pray the LORD my soul to take. Amen.

As I grew, I thought this was a *terrible* prayer. It caused me to question whether or not I'd be alive by morning and what was lurking under my bed to bring on my demise. I sort of threw it out there – and God understood.

Now let's transform it with Psalm 3.

*"Oh LORD, how are they increased that trouble me! Many are they that rise up against me. Many there are that say of my soul, 'there's no help for him in God.' But thou, O LORD, art a shield for me; my glory, and the lifter up of my head. I cried to the LORD with my voice, and he heard me out of his holy hill. **I lay down and slept; I woke up; for the LORD sustained me.** I will not be afraid of ten thousands of people that have set themselves against me round about. Arise, O LORD; save me, O my God: for you have smitten all my enemies upon the cheek bone; you have broken the teeth of the ungodly. Salvation belongs to the LORD: your blessing is upon your people."*

Psalm 3 KJV

As you make this your prayer and commit it to memory, remember God's word will be faithful to complete the work he's sent it to do. What does that mean? You will have the same peace as the sheep in the 23rd Psalm. You will lie down and sleep peacefully. Your focus will move away from yourself and draw comfort in YHVH, your refuge. God will save you – and bless you!

GOD'S WORD IS FAITHFUL	*"Be confident of this very thing, that he which hath begun a good work in you will perform it until the day of Jesus Christ..."*

Philippians 1:6 KJV

ALWAYS BE JOYFUL. NEVER STOP PRAYING. BE THANKFUL IN ALL CIRCUMSTANCES, FOR THIS IS GOD'S WILL FOR YOU WHO BELONG TO CHRIST JESUS.

DO NOT STIFLE THE HOLY SPIRIT. DO NOT SCOFF AT PROPHECIES, BUT TEST EVERYTHING THAT IS SAID. HOLD ON TO WHAT IS GOOD. STAY AWAY FROM EVERY KIND OF EVIL.

NOW MAY THE GOD OF PEACE MAKE YOU HOLY IN EVERY WAY, AND MAY YOUR WHOLE SPIRIT AND SOUL AND BODY BE KEPT BLAMELESS UNTIL OUR LORD JESUS CHRIST COMES AGAIN. GOD WILL MAKE THIS HAPPEN, FOR HE WHO CALLS YOU IS FAITHFUL.

1 THESSALONIANS 5:16-24 NLT

Build a Prayer

"… And in the morning, rising up a great while before day, he went out, and departed into a solitary place, and there prayed……"

Mark 1:35 KJV

Planning an *effective* prayer is a process. It forces you to take time away from the stress of the world and build quiet time both to think and to listen. What do you *really* want from God?

Personally, I've never been one to ask God to watch over me. Oh no, not me. If I have a request for the Creator of the Universe it's usually because I need help. The last thing I want is for him to sit there and watch me. I want *action*! I want answers! I want him to rescue me and pull me up out of the hole I just dug for myself. I want healing and wisdom and direction and anointing and financial abundance. But then again, I seem to dig more holes than most folks.

As you begin to visualize God's face focusing on you as you come to him with your request, knowing he's listening intently to every word coming out of your mouth, you'll want your words to have impact and be actionable.

And I guarantee as you build your prayer relationship with God you will begin to understand why Jesus used the seed comparison in Matthew 13. It's difficult. There will be times of frustration, weariness, procrastination, and times you simply won't be in the mood. Believe it or not, this is progress! Stand firm! Every time you get one inch closer to God, Satan will remind you of one more excuse why "now" just isn't a good time. Take a break, but don't give up. Grab a cup of coffee, come back, and take another bite out of The Manger.

Each prayer, each conversation you have with God will build your spirit. Physically you may not notice, but you will become stronger one prayer at a time.

<u>First</u>, what is needed or wanted from God *must* be established.

Write it down. Is it money? Not necessarily? The thinking process will prompt a decision – *is money more important than happiness, or is money happiness, or is money coming between our relationships with God?* To discover the need, try to pinpoint the problem beneath it. The root problem may be discipline or a health issue or even an image issue. If you're having trouble isolating the problem, ask God to show it to you. Then listen when he reveals it to you.

<u>Second</u>, take responsibility for the problem – whatever it is. Don't blame anyone else *(if you have trouble with this one, re-read the story of Adam and Eve and Cain in Genesis)*. Check out options. Get help. Find an accountability partner, but in your mind, own it. Why? Because if you don't own it, it isn't yours to give away. And God loves a cheerful giver.

GIVE IT TO GOD!	*"Each man should give what he has decided in his heart to give, not reluctantly or under compulsion, for God loves a cheerful giver."* *2 Corinthians 9:7 NIV*

<u>Third</u>, check out God's opinion. Before asking, research his publications on the subject. Where do we start? Of course – God's word!

*"For **the love of money** is a root of all sorts of evil, and some by longing for it have wandered away from the faith and pierced themselves with many griefs."* *1 Timothy 6:10 NASB*	**MONEY**

CHOICE	*"No one can serve two masters. Either he will hate the one and love the other, or he will be devoted to the one and despise the other. You cannot serve both God and Money."* *Matthew 6:24 NIV*

God's word is our standard. It is our plumb line. *(A plumb line is what a builder would use to insure an accurate, straight line.)* Remember <u>who</u> is God's word.

> *"This is what he showed me: The LORD was standing by a wall that had been built true to plumb, with a plumb line in his hand. And the LORD asked me, 'What do you see, Amos?'*
>
> *'A plumb line,' I replied.*
>
> *Then the LORD said, 'Look, I am setting a plumb line among my people Israel; I will spare them no longer.'"*
>
> *Amos 7:7–8 NIV*

PLUMB LINE

CALL HIM!

> *"Call Me, and I will answer you, and show you great and mighty things, which you do not know."* Jeremiah 33:3

Calling on the name of the Lord is a privilege and releases power into your life. So be intentional. Schedule time alone with God on a regular basis. It's helpful to keep an open Bible on your lap. Turn to Psalm 104, Psalm 136, Nehemiah 9 or Acts 7 as a starting place. These chapters provide a background of the character of God. If a verse stands out to you, ask God what it means to others, to you and to God. You have questions, so ask, one at a time. After each question, give God time to respond. Your answer may not be immediate but ask God to reveal it to you. Watch and listen for the answer.

Then jot down your prayerful *requests* and put a date by each one. When your request has been answered, jot down that date as well. It will benefit your spirit and your confidence in God will grow. Use Jesus' template in Matthew 6 to build your prayer. Remember to close your prayer using the power words – *in the Name of Jesus, by the Power of the Holy Spirit, and the Blood of the Lamb! Or just in the Name of Jesus.* Read John 14:13-14.

God is an expert on every subject. He holds the standard. He offers wisdom and advice from Genesis to Revelation. Soak up as much as possible daily.

Above all, remember – prayer is a conversation with God. There will be many times your conversation with God will only include one or two segments. There may be times your conversation with God won't include any of them. Sometimes it may be a one-word prayer, i.e., "HELP!" or "JESUS!" It's ok. He's your Father. Parents don't expect their children to carry on a professional conversation at 3 years of age. Allow God to mold your prayers through your continued time with him. Did I mention he's a great teacher? And he loves you! Just open your heart to him.

Remember, the Lord is coming soon. *"Don't worry about anything; instead, pray about everything. Tell God what you need and thank him for all he has done. If you do this, you will experience God's peace, which is far more wonderful than the human mind can understand. His peace will guard your hearts and minds as you live in Christ Jesus."* Philippians 4:6-7 NLV

"Behold, I am coming quickly! Blessed is he who keeps the words of the prophecy of this book." Revelation 22:7 NKJV

GOD'S CHARACTER

- *Father*
- *Heavenly Father*
- *My Lord and My God*
- *Merciful God*
- *YHVH (YAHveh)*
- *Alpha and Omega*
- *Righteous God*
- *My Rock*
- *Bread of Heaven*
- *My Sword*
- *Eternal Life*
- *Cornerstone*
- *Shepherd*
- *Lamb*
- *Eternal Word*
- *God of Warrior Hosts*
- *My Judge*
- *My Refuge*
- *Strong Tower*
- *Beloved of my Soul*
- *My Exceeding Joy*
- *My Buckler*
- *My Defense*
- *My Creator*
- *Sure Foundation*
- *My Power*
- *Living Water*
- *My Salvation*
- *God of Abraham*
- *Comforter*
- *God of Israel*
- *God of Knowledge*
- *Creator and Sustainer*

- *Almighty God*
- *My Provider*
- *My Healer*
- *My Savior*
- *My God*
- *My Helper*
- *Most High God*
- *Wise God*
- *Beginning & The End*
- *Alef and Tav*
- *My Bridegroom*
- *Deliverer*
- *Comforter*
- *Faithful God*
- *Glorious Lord*
- *Great God*
- *Light of the World*
- *My Hiding Place*
- *My Hope*
- *My Lamp*
- *My Portion*
- *My Praise*
- *King of Kings*
- *Maker of Heaven & Earth*
- *My Shield*
- *Marvelous God*
- *Consuming Fire*
- *Self-Existing God*
- *Jealous God*
- *High Priest*
- *My Scepter*
- *Restorer*
- *Horn of Salvation*

- *Eternal God*
- *King of Peace*
- *Adonai*
- *I AM*
- *Most Holy Lord*
- *Emmanuel*
- *Wonderful Counselor*
- *My Tower*
- *Beginning and End*
- *My Strength*
- *Eternal King*
- *First and Last*
- *My Maker*
- *Awesome God*
- *My Potter*
- *Refreshing River*
- *God of Grace*
- *King of Glory*
- *Lion of Judah*
- *Elohim*
- *Life-giver*
- *Redeemer*
- *Anointed One*
- *All Sufficient*
- *Father of Glory*
- *Father of Lights*
- *Strong Tower*
- *Author and Finisher*
- *Bright & Morning Star*
- *My Sure Foundation*
- *God of Mercy*
- *My Shelter*
- *Bread of Life*

I ask all these things in Jesus' name because it is written. If you abide in me and my words abide in you, you can ask whatever you will, and it shall be done to you.

Thank you for all you do for each one of your children. Keep them in your heart, tuck them under your wings, and cover them with your feathers.

Amen

PRAISE HIM!

God is listening to your heart. Your reaction to God's greatness, as he has shown it to you, is your praise. He knows how much you love him, but loves to hear it over and over and over again. **Praise him!** Don't be bashful. Was that a fabulous sunrise? Is he the most magnificent artist you've ever known? Thank him. Be creative – *reflect his image* – he created it all for you!

- *Lord, you are worthy to be praised!*

- *Lord, I sing praises to your name!*

- *You, O Lord, are my rock and my redeemer! You are my refuge!*

- *You are holy. Your praise shall continually be in my mouth!*

- *You, O Lord, are peace and blessing!*

- *You are my redeemer and king, the sovereign God!*

- *You are merciful, holy and powerful!*

- *You are my refuge, my fortress, my strong tower!*

- *You are the irresistible God who makes the nations tremble!*

- *You are my tremendous creator, maker of every living thing!*

- *You are ever-forgiving; you are my provider!*

- *You are the abaser and exalter; you are the giver of honor and the giver of dishonor!*

- *You are magnificent, infinite, and majestic, O LORD!*

- *I ponder all your great works and think about what you have done. I lift my hands to you in praise. I thirst for you as parched land thirsts for rain.*

- *Let all that I am praise the LORD. I will praise you, LORD, as long as I live. I will sing praises to my God with my dying breath. Joyful are those who have the God of Israel as their helper, whose hope is in the LORD their God. You made heaven and earth, the sea, and everything in them. You keep every promise forever. You give justice to the oppressed and food to the hungry. You, O LORD, free the prisoners. You, O LORD, open the eyes of the blind. You, O LORD, lift up those who are weighed down. You, O LORD, love the godly. You, O LORD, protect the foreigners among us. You, O LORD, care for the orphans and widows, but you frustrate the plans of the wicked. I will praise your Holy name!*

- *LORD, you will reign forever! You are my God throughout the generations. Praise the LORD!*

- *Praise the LORD! Praise the LORD from the heavens! Praise him from the skies! Praise him, all his angels! Praise him, all the armies of heaven! Praise him, sun and moon! Praise him, all you twinkling stars! Praise him, skies above! Praise him, vapors high above the clouds! Let every created thing give praise to the LORD, for he issued his command, and they came into being. He set them in place forever and ever. His decree will never be revoked.*

- *Praise the LORD! How good to sing praises to our God! How delightful and how fitting! You heal the brokenhearted and bandage their wounds. You count the stars and call them all by name. How great are you, LORD! Your power is absolute! Your understanding is beyond comprehension! LORD, you support the humble, but bring the wicked down into the dust. I sing thanks to you LORD! You cover the heavens with clouds, provide rain for the earth, and make the grass grow in mountain pastures. You give food to the wild animals and feed the young ravens when they cry. You take no pleasure in the strength of a horse or in human might. No, the LORD's delight is in those who fear him, those who put their hope in his unfailing love. Glorify the LORD, O Jerusalem! Praise your God, O Zion! For he has strengthened the bars of your gates and blessed your children within your walls. He sends peace across your nation and satisfies your hunger with the finest wheat. He sends his orders to the world—how swiftly his word flies! He sends the snow like white wool; he scatters frost upon the ground like ashes. He hurls the hail like stones. Who can stand against his freezing cold? Then, at his command, it all melts. He sends his winds, and the ice thaws. He has revealed his words to Jacob, his decrees and regulations to Israel. He has not done this for any other nation; they do not know his regulations. Praise the LORD! PRAISE THE LORD!*

- *Praise the LORD from the earth, you creatures of the ocean depths, fire and hail, snow and clouds, wind and weather that obey him, mountains and all hills, fruit trees and all cedars, wild animals and all livestock, small scurrying animals and birds, kings of the earth and all people, rulers and judges of the earth, young men and young women, old men and children.*

107

- *Let everything that has breath praise the name of the LORD! Your name is very great; your glory towers over the earth and heaven! You have made your people strong, honoring your faithful ones who are close to you. Praise the LORD!*

- *Let all that I am praise the LORD. I will praise the LORD as long as I live. I will sing praises to my God with my dying breath. Don't let me put confidence in powerful people; there is no help for me there. When they breathe their last, they return to the earth, and all their plans die with them. But joyful are those who have the God of Israel as their helper, whose hope is in the LORD their God. Father, you made heaven and earth, the sea, and everything in them. You keep every promise forever. You give justice to the oppressed and food to the hungry. You free the prisoners. You open the eyes of the blind. You lift up those who are weighed down. You love the godly. You protect the foreigners among us. You care for the orphans and widows, but you frustrate the plans of the wicked.*

REPENT!

Offer true **repentance**. Repent simply means, 'stop where you are and turn around.' If you're not obeying God's word, stop where you are, turn around and obey. If you're not walking with God, stop where you are, turn around, figure it out, and walk with God. If you have no relationship with God, stop where you are, turn around and build your relationship. Not for a moment, not for a day, not for a week, not for a year, but always.

Some segment samples are from scripture. They're very easy to spot, aren't they? All of our words to the Father are important to him. However, prayers from ***God's word*** carry deeper impact. This is not an accident. God's word is powerful. Yes, God wants to hear from your heart. But he also wants you to experience the power that comes from speaking *His Word*. When we're drawn to his word and commit it to memory and speak it out loud in his image, God moves forward with his plan for our lives!

And yes, when we simply cry out to our Father, *"I'm so sorry, please forgive me!"* he is quick to forgive. There is no wrong way to offer our repentance!

- *Father, forgive me!*

- *Father, I'm so sorry I haven't been searching for you. Help me turn my life around and focus on you!*

- *Father, I'm your child and I'm in desperate need of a forgiving father. Hold me, forgive me, share your wisdom and show me how to walk with you.*

- *Father, erase my sin; bury it deep in a faraway ocean and don't let me find it again.*

- *Purify me from my sins, and I will be clean; wash me, and I will be whiter than snow. Oh, give me back my joy again; you have broken me—now let me rejoice. Don't keep looking at my sins.*

- *Have mercy on me, O God, because of your unfailing love. Because of your great compassion, blot out the stain of my sins. Wash me clean from my guilt. Purify me from my sin. I recognize my rebellion; it haunts me day and night. Against you, and you alone, have I sinned; I have done what is evil in your sight. You will be proved right in what you say, and your judgment against me is just. For I was born a sinner—yes, from the moment my mother conceived me. But you desire honesty from the womb, teaching me wisdom even there.*

- *Remove the stain of my guilt. Create in me a clean heart, O God. Renew a loyal spirit within me. Do not banish me from your presence, and don't take your Holy Spirit from me.*

- *Restore to me the joy of your salvation, and make me willing to obey you. Then I will teach your ways to rebels, and they will return to you. Forgive me for shedding blood, O God who saves; then I will joyfully sing of your forgiveness. Unseal my lips, O LORD, that my mouth may praise you.*

- *Forgive all my sins and heal all my diseases.*

- *Help me turn to you, LORD, and have mercy on me. Forgive me generously.*

- *Forgive all my sins and graciously receive me, so that I may offer you praises from the depth of my heart.*

- *Your blood, Father, which confirms the covenant between you and your people, is poured out as a sacrifice to forgive the sins of many. Forgive me and allow your blood to saturate my heart and soul.*

- *Forgive me, Father, for you have said, "If we confess our sins to him, he is faithful and just to forgive us our sins and to cleanse us from all wickedness." LORD, I lay my sins before you. Wipe them away out of my sight and fill me with your holiness. Teach me to walk with you in your precepts and learn from your wisdom. Use me in your kingdom, LORD, I want to serve you.*

MAKE YOUR *REQUESTS* KNOWN

One day Jesus told his disciples a story to show that they should always pray and never give up. "There was a judge in a certain city," he said, "who neither feared God nor cared about people. A widow of that city came to him repeatedly, saying, 'Give me justice in this dispute with my enemy.' The judge ignored her for a while, but finally he said to himself, 'I don't fear God *or* care about people, but this woman is driving me crazy. I'm going to see that she gets justice, because she is wearing me out with her constant requests!'"

Then the LORD said, *"Learn a lesson from this unjust judge. Even he rendered a just decision in the end. So don't you think God will surely give justice to his chosen people who **cry out to him day***

and night? *Will he keep putting them off? I tell you, he will grant justice to them quickly! But when the Son of Man returns, how many will he find on the earth who have faith?" (Luke 18:1-8 NLT)*

Again, God is teaching us. Don't just flippantly ask once and never mention it again, if you're serious, stay with it and in faith, keep asking over and over. We can't see what's taking place in spiritual places. The 10th chapter of Daniel reveals an angel telling Daniel his prayers had been heard, but that Satan had been fighting against this angel for three weeks before the warrior angel, Michael, came to help him.

"Then he [angel] *said to me, "Do not be afraid, Daniel, for from the first day that you set your heart on understanding this and on humbling yourself before your God, your words were heard, and I have come in response to your words. But the prince of the kingdom of Persia was withstanding me for twenty-one days; then behold, Michael, one of the chief princes, came to help me, for I had been left there with the kings of Persia." (Daniel 10:12-13 NASB)*

Stay the course!

- *Father, in Luke 11:9 KJV, you said, "Ask, and it shall be given you; seek, and ye shall find; knock, and it shall be opened unto you." LORD, I've come before you asking, seeking, and knocking. LORD, welcome me into your presence, cleanse me and make me whole.*

- *Father, in John 14:13-14 NKJV, Jesus said, "…whatever you ask in my name, that will I do, that the Father may be glorified in the Son. If you ask anything in my name, I will do it." Father, I ask for healing – physically, mentally, emotionally, spiritually and financially in the name of Jesus, that you, Father, will be glorified in the Son!*

- *I come to you for protection, O LORD my God. Save me from my persecutors – rescue me! If you don't they will maul me like a lion, tearing me to pieces with no one to rescue me.*

- *Father, my heart longs to reflect your image. Give me wisdom. Show me how to walk with you.*

111

- *You O Lord, are our sun and our shield. Your give us grace and glory. The Lord will withhold no good thing from those who do what is right.*

- *Lord, I call financial abundance, according to your word in Luke 6:38, "because I have given, it shall be given unto me – good measure, pressed down, shaken together and running over, shall men give into my bosom."* (Notice a record of giving must have occurred.)

- *Lord, Just burst through the heavens and come down! When you came down long, long ago, you did awesome things beyond our wildest expectations – and oh, how the mountains shook! Come with your Holy Spirit and cover me with the precious healing blood of the lamb. Saturate every cell in my body with your cleansing. I call health and healing into my body and I call out sickness and disease in the name of Jesus, by the power of the Holy Spirit and the Blood of the Lamb because, 'he was wounded for our transgressions, he was bruised for our iniquities: the chastisement for our peace was upon him; and by his stripes we are healed. Just as the blueness of a wound cleanses away evil: so do stripes the inward parts.' Sickness and disease, get out! Get out in the name of Jesus! Health and Healing, COME! Come quickly and cleanse every cell. Thank you, Jesus, for the stripes you bore for my healing.*

- *Lord, I call health and healing into my body. In Romans 4:17, you said to call those things which are not as though they were. Although it feels like my body is sick and damaged, I call health and healing into it in the name of Jesus, by the power of the Holy Spirit and the blood of the precious Lamb.*

- *Father, I trust you. In Philippians 4:19 KJV your word says, "My God shall supply all your need according to his riches in glory by Christ Jesus."* Teach me to have faith. Teach me to walk with you. Father, supply all my need according to your riches in glory by Christ Jesus!

"And all these blessings shall come upon you, and overtake you, if you obey and listen to the voice of the LORD your God."   *Deuteronomy 28:2 NKJV*

WHAT GOD WANTS

What is your ministry? Jesus said to pray, *"Thy kingdom come. Thy will be done on earth, as it is in heaven."* Let's hover here for just a minute. Again, God is teaching us *how* to reflect his image.

Jesus said, *"How can I describe the Kingdom of God? What story should I use to illustrate it? It is like a mustard seed planted in the ground. It is the smallest of all seeds, but it becomes the largest of all garden plants; it grows long branches, and birds can make nests in its shade."*[9]

What is so special about this mustard seed? Just like the rest of creation *(outside of man)* it is obedient to God's command. It doesn't whine because it's so little, or because it isn't a fruit tree seed or an eagle. No! It understands its role. It knows deep inside that it is destined to become great. And not only will it become great through all the storms of life, it will also provide protection and comfort for others in God's creation.

Jesus also said, *"The Kingdom of God is like a farmer who scatters seed on the ground. Night and day, while he's asleep or awake, the seed sprouts and grows, but he does not understand how it happens. The earth produces the crops on its own. First a leaf blade pushes through, then the heads of wheat are formed, and finally the grain ripens. And as soon as the grain is ready, the farmer comes and harvests it with a sickle, for the harvest time has come."*[10]

Now Jesus is the *farmer* scattering seeds on the ground. Are you with me? You and I are the seeds, and we grow according to the type of soil into which we fall. Remember the parable of the sower? God plants seeds (us) in his word. He surrounds us with it on all sides. Our reaction to his word (Jesus) determines our end. If we embrace the soil (God's word) and dig deep like the mustard seed, we will fulfill our purpose because we know deep within us that we are destined to become great.

---

[9] Mark 4:30-32 NLT
[10] *Mark 4:26-29 NLT*

God teaches many things in one parable. *[Father – you truly are amazing! Thank you!]* We could build and build and take off in several directions. In some ways, we're like the farmer. We don't understand how all this works. We don't understand how God causes us (his seeds) to grow, but the mustard seed understands. It has one goal – to fulfill its role and purpose while giving glory to God.

"But if I am casting out demons by the Spirit of God, then the Kingdom of God has arrived among you," Jesus said in Matthew 12:28 NLT.   Hhmm…

In addition to God, the Word, the Truth, and the Way, Jesus is *also* the Kingdom of God.

"I tell you the truth, anyone who doesn't receive the Kingdom of God like a child will never enter it."[11]

"Thy kingdom come. Thy will be done on earth, as it is in heaven." Jesus is instructing us to plead for God's kingdom to come into our lives so that we will fulfill our purpose on earth with faith and determination as we reflect the image of God as he is in heaven. We have been given the Word of God *(Jesus)* to carry to the nations. We are the hands and feet of Jesus. We are to reflect the image of God's heavenly SOP[12], only here on earth. We are to go and tell the nations. We are to lift up one another with the word. We are to call those things that are not as though they were!

Be the mustard seed. *Reflect the image of God.* Chew on it awhile.

- *Let each generation tell its children of your mighty acts; let them proclaim your power. I will meditate on your majestic, glorious splendor and your wonderful miracles. Your awe-inspiring deeds will be on every tongue; I will proclaim your greatness. Everyone will share the story of your wonderful goodness; they will sing with joy about your righteousness.*

- *Father, draw my children close to you. LORD, feed them with the heritage of Jacob as they obey your word. Hide it in their hearts that they might not sin against you. Capture them by your*

---

[11] Luke 18:17 NLT
[12] standard operating procedures

Holy Spirit and protect them from the evil one. Love them, lead them, and guide them by your light. Give them wisdom, peace, joy, love, mercy and grace that they will walk with you all the days of their lives and they will dwell in the house of the LORD forever. I ask it all in Jesus' name, by the power of the Holy Spirit and the blood of the Lamb!

- *LORD, touch hearts all across the world. Draw them by your Holy Spirit. Teach them your word. Meet their needs, O LORD, that they will call upon your name and exalt you with thanksgiving. Bring revival through your Holy Spirit, LORD, in Jesus' name.*

- *LORD, I pray for peace in Jerusalem according to your command. Send your Holy Spirit to your people. Soften their hearts to receive your word. Teach them to walk with you. Protect them from the destroyer. Love them, lead them, and guide them in wisdom. I ask in Jesus' name, by the power of the Holy Spirit and the blood of the Lamb!*

- *Prepare me for battle. Anoint me with the Blood of Jesus; cover me completely and protect me from the evil one as I build my relationship with you, my commander, and carry your word to a lost world.*

- *LORD, fill us with your peace. Renew our hearts and minds with the refreshing of a mountain stream in spring. Send your Holy Spirit before us to draw hearts close to you. Use us each day as we minister to others, that we will be tall standing stones in your kingdom.*

Take time for prayer. Take time for praise. *Reflect the image* of those in whom you were created!

PRAISE!

Praise the LORD!

Praise God in his sanctuary; praise him in his mighty heavens!
Praise him for his mighty deeds;
Praise him according to his excellent greatness!

Praise him with trumpet sound; Praise him with lute and harp!
Praise him with tambourine and dance; praise him with strings and pipe!
Praise him with sounding cymbals; praise him with **loud** clashing cymbals! Let everything that has breath praise the LORD!

PRAISE THE LORD!

Psalm *150 NKJV*

Again, prayer is conversation. There are as many prayers as there are conversations. As you make a disciplined effort to get closer to God, Satan will attempt *whatever it takes* to steal your faith and kill your relationship. Hang in there!

In times of bondage – when you feel an oppressive spirit – repeat the precious name of Jesus over and over and over and ask him to cover you with his blood and protect you from the evil one. "*Jesus, Jesus*" Satan just hates that name!

In times when your prayers seem routine, and you're seeking God's powerful anointing, pray for others.

SCRIPTURE PRAYERS

The following paragraphs are prayers built upon the word of God. There are many, many more throughout the Bible. Search through the word and seal him upon your heart. Cling to him. He is life and health and healing.

Lord I cry out to you and plead for your mercy. I'm pouring out my complaints before you, and telling you all my troubles. When I am overwhelmed, you alone know the way I should turn. Wherever I go, my enemies have set traps for me. I look for someone to come and help me, but no one gives me a passing thought! No one will help me; no one cares a bit what happens to me. Then I pray to you, O Lord. I say, "You are my place of refuge. You are all I really want in life. Hear my cry, for I am very low. Rescue me from my persecutors, for they are too strong for me. Bring me out of prison so I can thank you. The godly will crowd around me, for you are good to me." Hear my prayer, O Lord; listen to my plea! Answer me because you are faithful and righteous. Don't put your servant on trial, for no one is innocent before you. My enemy has chased me. He has knocked me to the ground and forces me to live in darkness like those in the grave. I am losing all hope; I am paralyzed with fear. I remember the days of old. I ponder all your great works and think about what you have done. I lift my hands to you in praise. I thirst for you as parched land thirsts for rain.

I'm calling on you, O God, for you will answer me; give ear to me and hear my prayer. Show the wonder of your great love, you who save by your right hand those who take refuge in you from their foes. Keep me as the apple of your eye; hide me in the shadow of your wings from the wicked who assail me, from my mortal enemies who surround me. They close up their callous hearts, and their mouths speak with arrogance. They have tracked me down, they now surround me, with eyes alert, to throw me to the ground. They are like a lion hungry for prey, like a great lion crouching in cover. Rise up, O Lord, confront them, bring them down; rescue me from the wicked by your sword. O Lord, by your hand save me from such men, from men of this world whose reward is in this life. You still the hunger of those you cherish;

their sons have plenty, and they store up wealth for their children. And I—in righteousness I will see your face; when I awake, I will be satisfied with seeing your likeness.

Come quickly, LORD, and answer me, for my depression deepens. Don't turn away from me, or I will die. Let me hear of your unfailing love each morning, for I am trusting you. Show me where to walk, for I give myself to you. Rescue me from my enemies, LORD; I run to you to hide me. Teach me to do your will, for you are my God. May your gracious Spirit lead me forward on a firm footing. For the glory of your name, O LORD, preserve my life. Because of your faithfulness, bring me out of this distress.

Praise the LORD, who is my rock! You train my hands for war and give my fingers skill for battle. You are my loving ally and my fortress, my tower of safety, my rescuer. You are my shield, and I take refuge in you. Open the heavens, LORD, and come down. Touch the mountains so they billow smoke. Hurl your lightning bolts and scatter your enemies! Shoot your arrows and confuse them! Reach down from heaven and rescue me; rescue me from deep waters, from the power of my enemies. May our sons flourish in their youth like well-nurtured plants. May our daughters be like graceful pillars, carved to beautify a palace. May our barns be filled with crops of every kind. May the flocks in our fields multiply by the thousands, even tens of thousands, and may our oxen be loaded down with produce. May there be no enemy breaking through our walls, no going into captivity, no cries of alarm in our town squares. Yes, joyful are those who live like this! Joyful indeed are those whose God is the LORD. I will exalt you, my God and King, and praise your name forever and ever. I will praise you every day; yes, I will praise you forever. Great is the LORD! He is most worthy of praise! No one can measure his greatness.

The LORD is merciful and compassionate, slow to get angry and filled with unfailing love. LORD, you are good to everyone. You shower compassion on all your creation. All of your works will thank you, LORD, and your faithful followers will praise you. They will speak of the glory of your kingdom; they will give examples of your power. They will tell about your mighty deeds and about the majesty and glory of your reign. For your kingdom is an everlasting kingdom. You rule throughout all generations. You always keep your promises; you are gracious in all you do. You help the fallen and lift those bent beneath their loads. The eyes of all look to you in hope; you give them their food as they need it. When you open your hand, you satisfy the hunger and thirst of every living thing. You are righteous in everything you do; you are filled with kindness. You are close to all who call on you, yes, to all who call on you in truth. Father, you grant the desires of those who fear you; you hear their cries for help and rescue them. You protect all those who love you, but you destroy the wicked. I will praise you LORD, and may everyone on earth bless his holy name forever and ever. Praise the LORD!

LORD, please just burst through the clouds and come down! Oh, how the nations would tremble! Just like fire causes wood to burn and water to boil, so your coming would cause all the nations to tremble; and oh, how the mountains would quake! When you came down long, long ago, you did awesome things beyond our highest expectations – and oh, how the mountains quaked! Since the beginning of time, not one ear has heard and not one eye has seen a God like you, who works for those who wait for him.

We're waiting for you now, Father, to show us your plan for our lives. Minister among us; fill our empty vessels with the tools you would have us to pour out upon your people: love, joy, peace, mercy, comfort, grace, wisdom, healing, compassion, patience, faith, goodness and honesty.

We are confident of this one thing – that you have already begun a good work in us and will continue to work it out in our lives until your precious son, Jesus the Christ, the holy one, the pure Lamb of God, comes back again to receive us unto himself.

Take us by the hand; lead us by your Spirit; teach us to walk with you, in Jesus' name. AMEN.

This book is merely an introduction to communicating with your eternal Father. It is up to you to build your relationship, to experience joy, healing, peace, grace, love and mercy. Take his hand. Follow his lead. Meditate on his Word both day and night.

In sharing my heart, I trust you will have gleaned some meaningful morsels to chew on. Your words will heal or hurt. The choice is yours. I pray you choose God and his Word. While an intimate, personal relationship with YHVH requires hard work and commitment, remember the imminent war waging against your spirit. God has provided the foundation for you to stand upon. Gear up for the battle!

'If you turn from him and embrace the world…'

God will act upon your life and your requests, according to your words. What happens if you decide not to follow Jesus, not to walk with God?

"If a person does not repent, God will sharpen his sword; he will bend and string his bow. He will prepare his deadly weapons and shoot his flaming arrows." Psalm 7:12-13 NLT

"You can enter God's Kingdom only through the narrow gate. The highway to hell is broad, and its gate is wide for the many who choose that way. But the gateway to life is very narrow and the road is difficult, and only a few ever find it."

Matthew 7:13-14 NLT

> **CHOOSE**
> **YOUR**
> **PATH**
> **WISELY**

Paul's passionate letter to the Romans ends with the following report about the future of Satan and his followers:

"…The God of peace will soon crush Satan under your feet. May the grace of our LORD Jesus be with you."[13]

---

[13] Romans 16:20 NLT

The End

UNDERSTAND THREE THINGS

1. SATAN IS DEFEATED – BY JESUS

"He [Jesus] canceled the record of the charges against us and took it away by nailing it to the cross. In this way, he disarmed the spiritual rulers and authorities. He shamed them publicly by his victory over them on the cross."[14]

Satan has been decisively defeated through the death and resurrection of Christ. This decisive blow nailed repentant sins upon the cross of Christ, canceling all records of charges against us. The one and only weapon with which Satan still can damn people is through unforgiven sin.

2. SATAN IS DEFEATED – BY ARMOR-BEARING CHRISTIANS

Christians defeat Satan daily when they wield the sword of God's word and put on the whole armor of God. Satan is powerless against the power of the word and the blood of Jesus.

3. SATAN IS DEFEATED – AND DESTROYED

"Then I saw an angel coming down from heaven with the key to the bottomless pit and a heavy chain in his hand. He seized the dragon—that old serpent, who is the devil, Satan—and bound him in chains for a thousand years. The angel threw him into the bottomless pit, which he then shut and locked so Satan could not deceive the nations anymore until the thousand years were finished. Afterward he must be released for a little while.

"Then I saw thrones, and the people sitting on them had been given the authority to judge. And I saw the souls of those who had been beheaded for their testimony about Jesus and for proclaiming the word of God. They had not worshiped the beast or his statue, nor accepted his mark on their forehead or their hands. They all came to life again, and they reigned with Christ for a thousand years.

"This is the first resurrection. (The rest of the dead did not come back to life until the thousand years had ended.) Blessed and holy are those who share in the first resurrection. For them the

---

[14] Colossians 2:14-15 NLT

second death holds no power, but they will be priests of God and of Christ and will reign with him a thousand years.

"When the thousand years come to an end, Satan will be let out of his prison. Then the devil, who had deceived them, was thrown into the fiery lake of burning sulfur, joining the beast and the false prophet. There they will be tormented day and night forever and ever. Then I saw a great white throne and him who was seated on it. Earth and sky fled from his presence, and there was no place for them. And I saw the dead, great and small, standing before the throne, and books were opened. Another book was opened, which is the book of life. The dead were judged according to what they had done as recorded in the books. The sea gave up the dead that were in it, and death and Hades gave up the dead that were in them, and each person was judged according to what he had done. Then death and Hades were thrown into the lake of fire. The lake of fire is the second death. If anyone's name was not found written in the book of life, he was thrown into the lake of fire."[15]

"Whatever is in your heart determines what you say. A good person produces good things from the treasury of a good heart, and an evil person produces evil things from the treasury of an evil heart. And I tell you this, you must give an account on judgment day for every idle word you speak. The words you say will either acquit you or condemn you."

Matthew 12:34b-37 NLT

> **YOUR WORDS WILL CHOOSE WHOM YOU WILL SERVE**

"The people surrounded Jesus and asked, "How long are you going to keep us in suspense? If you are the Messiah, tell us plainly."

---

[15] Revelation 20:1-7,10-15 NLT

Jesus replied, *"I have already told you, and you don't believe me. The proof is the work I do in my Father's name. But you don't believe me because you are not my sheep. My sheep listen to my voice; I know them, and they follow me. I give them eternal life, and they will never perish."*[16]

THE END	*"Whoever believes in the Son has eternal life, but whoever rejects the Son will not see life, for God's wrath remains on him."*

John 3:36 NIV

"Those who are dominated by the sinful nature think about sinful things, but those who are controlled by the Holy Spirit think about things that please the Spirit. So letting your sinful nature control your mind leads to death. But letting the Spirit control your mind leads to life and peace. For the sinful nature is always hostile to God. It never did obey God's laws, and it never will. That's why those who are still under the control of their sinful nature can never please God."[17] *"When people keep on sinning, it shows that they belong to the devil, who has been sinning since the beginning."*[18]

"Not everyone who calls out to me, 'Lord! Lord!' will enter the Kingdom of Heaven. Only those who actually do the will of my Father in heaven will enter. On judgment day many will say to me, 'Lord! Lord! We prophesied in your name and cast out demons in your name and performed many miracles in your name.' But I will reply, 'I never knew you."	**BUILD YOUR RELATIONSHIP!**

Matthew 7:21-23a NLT

"For this reason also, since the day we heard of it, we have not ceased to pray for you and to ask that you may be filled with the knowledge of His will in all spiritual wisdom and understanding,

---

[16] John 10:24-28
[17] Romans 8:5-8
[18] *1 John 3:8a NLT*

so that you will walk in a manner worthy of the LORD, to please Him in all respects, bearing fruit in every good work and increasing in the knowledge of God; strengthened with all power, according to His glorious might, for the attaining of all steadfastness and patience; joyously giving thanks to the Father, who has qualified us to share in the inheritance of the saints in Light."[19]

Show me in God's word where it says following Christ is safe. Show me in God's word where it says following Christ is easy, or there is no risk, or no battle. Show me in God's word where it says following Christ isn't dangerous, or doesn't cost you something, or *everything*. Redefine your vision of God, build your relationship, find your purpose, and reflect his image!

"For all creation is waiting eagerly for that future day when God will reveal who his children really are."

Romans 8:19 NLT

---

[19] Colossians 1:9-12 NASB

p.s. Don't forget to floss your teeth.

I love you.

ABOUT THE AUTHOR

My life's journey from desperation to abundance has provided great insight into the marvelous and mysterious power of prayer.

I am a sinner saved by grace. And like many, I've been broken, abused and crushed. I've sold my only watch to buy food for my son. I've experienced that diet of one good meal every three days, and endured months in a dingy, odor-filled basement.

It's called 'sheep school' and I'm blessed to have experienced brokenness. While alone on the hilly-side of my life, my Shepard molded my will to his own. He continues to teach me to walk at his side and raise little sheep of my own.

If you're broken or abused or can't find your purpose, this book is for you. If your life is a blessing but you long for a more powerful prayer life, this book is for you. If you've never prayed because you don't know what to say, this book is for you.

"The LORD looks down from heaven on the sons of men to see if there are any who understand, any who seek God." Psalm 14:2 NLV

Seek God and be blessed!

Printed in the United States
by Baker & Taylor Publisher Services